Dynamic Song Performance

The Singer's Bible

By Pepper Jay

with contributions by

John Michael Ferrari

DYNAMIC SONG PERFORMANCE
A Singer's Bible

By Pepper Jay

Original material copyright 2016
Pepper Jay Productions LLC
ISBN 978-0-692-26839-1
ISBN-10:0692268391

WGA# 1514999

Printed in the United States of America
www.PepperJay.com

First Edition

No part of the original material contained in this book may be reproduced or transmitted in any form or by any means, electronic or mechanical, including photocopying, recording, or by any information storage and retrieval system, without permission in writing from the publisher.

Published worldwide.

Address all queries
c/o Pepper Jay
Pepper Jay Productions LLC
2300 Postal Road
5125
Pahrump, NV 89060

Cover photo of Danika Quinn
By John Wright

Back cover photo of Pepper Jay
By John Michael Ferrari

Acknowledgements

I owe much of my success to the extraordinary efforts and devotion of my students and to the creativity and suggestions of my production partner, John Michael Ferrari.

I especially appreciate my students' continued trust.

I also give thanks:

To G-d, the beginning of everything.

To Allison Iraheta, Nikki Nova, Golda Berkman, Brandon James, Giselle, Stevie Wright, and Montana Tucker for show-casing to the world how far **Dynamic Song Performance** skills can take devoted talents desiring to make singing performance their career.

To my son and mentor, John Robert Palacio, without whom none of my achievements would be as successful.

To Thurston Watts, may he rest in peace, for sharing the excitement and joy of song performance.

To Al Boyd, Rebecca Kyler Downs, Fancy, Allison Iraheta, Brandon James, Kenyatta Mackey, Laura Martin, Danika Quinn, Susie Stillwell, Melinda del Toro, and the Associated Press for their assistance with the illustrative photos in this text. And, thank you to photographers John Michael Ferrari, John Wright, and Jeff Knight.

To Lisa Popeil (Voiceworks) for her invaluable insights.

In appreciation,

PepperJay

Contents

Preface……………………………………………………………………..viii

Welcome to *Dynamic Song Performance*………………………………… 1

Chapter One………………………………………………………………….6

General Information about Song Performance

- Section 1A   What Is Song Performance?…………………7
- Section 1B   What Are Song Performanc Skills?…………13
    - Song Performance Skills Toolbox
- Section 1C………………………………………………………..15
    - How Are Song Performan Skills Developed?
    - Learn your craft
    - Explore Your Inner Universe
    - Enjoy the Process

- Section 1D………………………………………………………20
    - What Is a Song Performance Coach?
    - How a Vocal Performance Coach Differs from a Vocal Teacher
    - Tips on How to Choose a Coach

Chapter Two…………………………………………………………………..24
How to DO IT!
- Section 2A   Audience Psychology Is EVERYTHING! …...25
    - No One Is a Stranger
    - Name Your Chair/ Own the Floor
- Section 2B   The Importance of an INTRA-Audience …….29
    Bond of Appreciation
- Section 2C   Be Sincere with your Lyrics…………………31
- Section 2D   Be Sincere with Your Patter………………..34
- Section 2E   Will Them to Look at You……………………36
    - Don't Abandon Your Audience
    - Experience Your Audience/ Come Back to Me
    - Don't Sing to Yourself

- Section 2F The Camera Is one of Your Audience...........**40**
    Members
    -Stimulate from All Sides
    -Serious Subjects
    -The Three Step Punch

Chapter Three...**46**
Communicate Your Song
- Section 3A Phrasing..**47**
- Section 3B Enunciation...**50**
- Section 3C Build the Song.......................................**53**
- Section 3D Vocal Performance Tips.........................**54**
- Section 3E Body Movement- Compliment the **62**
    Phrasing
    -Keep it Interesting
    -Blend of Physical and Vocal Communication
    -Congruence
    -Deaf Man's Introduction
    -End Freeze
    -Acknowledge Your Audience
- Section 3F It's All In Your Eyes and Facial Expressions...**69**
    -Eye Contact
    -Allow Your Face to Express the Lyrics

Chapter Four...**72**
How to Move On Stage
- Section 4A Stay Balanced..**73**
- Section 4B Move your Chi (aka: Pendulum Method)........**77**
- Section 4C How to Walk On Stage............................**81**
- Section 4D Introduce Yourself to Your Body..................**84**
- Section 4E Choreography- Create an Act....................**87**

Chapter Five..**90**
Package Yourself
- Section 5A Mimic Your Models................................**91**
- Section 5B Choose Your Style..................................**95**
- Section 5C Package Yourself as a Song Performer........**109**
- Section 5D Create a Fan Base................................**115**
- Section 5E Demo Reels... **117**
- Section 5F Pay Your Dues......................................**121**
- Section 5G Practice the Audition Process.................. **123**
- Section 5H Learn How to Be a Photograph.............. **128**

Conclusion..**132**
Appendices..**133**
Notes **156**

Dynamic Song Performance

Thurston Watts, Allison Iraheta,
John Michael Ferrari - Photo by Pepper Jay

Preface
By Allison Iraheta

Pepper Jay and John Michael Ferrari were my tag-team performance coaches from when I had just turned 12 years old until my 17th birthday. We trained at Pepper's studio in Hollywood, California (before it had air conditioning ... hot!). My sessions with Pepper and John were tailor-made specifically for me and their focus was always on what was required to achieve results toward my goals.

Pepper Jay produced John Michael Ferrari's "oldies" band, "Ferrari and Friends," and during those years, in addition to my studio lessons, I gained on-stage experience as the female lead singer performing with many experienced entertainers including Thurston Watts (may he rest in peace).

I remember the day in Pepper's studio when I saw her cry. We were rehearsing for my appearance on "American Idol" (Season 8). As I finished performing a song, Pepper, with tears rolling down her cheeks, said, "That! Do that and you will win 'American Idol.'" I remember how my big grin felt as well as my confidence. Well, maybe I didn't win, but I came close (Top 4, Season 8), and I continue my career today as the lead in the band, "Halo Circus," with my love Matt Hager. I owe much of my success to the loving and entertaining song performance coaching by Pepper Jay and John Michael Ferrari.

Thank you guys. You are family.

Dynamic Song Performance

Allison Iraheta & Matt Hager (Halo Circus)
at Pepper Jay's - Photo by Jeff Knight

Welcome to Dynamic Song Performance
The Singer's Bible!

Welcome to **Dynamic Song Performance**, a Singer's Bible. I believe this to be the only how-to performance book for singers that is equally valuable to magicians, comics, actors, public speakers, models, performance coaches, and trial lawyers. Why? Because I focus on audience psychology. I explain what every performer must do to seduce the camera and the audience, to keep the crowds enthralled, and turn listeners and viewers into loyal fans.

I enjoy teaching song performance skills to singers from all genres of music, from country to pop to rap to opera to musical theatre. I believe wonderful singers are great storytellers.

My singing students' ambitions vary from wowing friends as karaoke singers to dreams of succeeding as cabaret performers, nightclub acts, rock stars, recording artists, and/or contest winners, to actors who want to "book" singing roles in films and prime time TV.

Over three decades, I developed the Dynamic Song Performance method of teaching song performance skills. At first, I taught in public schools of the Los Angeles Unified School District. Later, I privately coached singers, including John Michael Ferrari. In the mid-90's, John joined me as my coaching partner.

I hope the skills in this **Dynamic Song Performance** text will help you better understand the elements of song performance so you may utilize your full potential when sharing your performance on stage, in front of cameras, and in a recording studio.

Dynamic Song Performance may also be of use to fellow song performance coaches, voice teachers, or talent mangers looking to refine their methods of coaching and expanding their understanding of the craft of song performance and client packaging.

Dynamic Song Performance should provide immediate results. My students quickly discover how comfortably and quickly they improve upon the technical, emotional, and psychological aspects of their craft; including voice, sound, movement, space, confidence, and audience psychology.

Learn to become "one" with your audience and begin to examine how audiences can enjoy magical moments vicariously through your singing performances.

Your improvement of any single performance skill will take you closer to a greatly improved performance. Do not wait until you have time to practice and learn all of the song performance skills I've included. Instead, read and apply the skills one at a time or a few at a time. Some performance skills will be new to you and others good reminders.

Dynamic Song Performance opens the door to different things for different people; whether a novice

or a professional entertainer. If one applies the skills in this text, you will:

- See the unique artist you're meant to be;
- weave a web of intimacy that keeps the audience on your side, even when a joke or a musical note falls flat;
- sound like an entertainment professional;
- project authenticity, sincerity, and believability;
- find out if unconscious mannerisms or facial expressions are working against you;

and,

- use your eyes, hand, body, voice, and facial expressions to bond completely with your audience.

On a personal note, as a child growing up in Hollywood, my Grandma Lida was my best friend and her best friend was Sophie Tucker – "Last of the Great Hot Mamas". I tagged along with show-biz family and friends to the Moulin Rouge, Coconut Grove, the Sahara and Flamingo Hotels in Las Vegas, etc, to enjoy masters like Frank Sinatra, Jimmy Durante, Dean Martin, and Sammy Davis Jr. weave that magical intimate circle around their audience. By the time I was five, I was charming my own audience with my tap dancing and accordion playing on stage and, soon after, enjoying acting in the theatre and in TV sitcoms.

Sophie Tucker to Lida Ardel (1959)

Now a performance coach for several decades, I have enjoyed helping singers, stand-up comics, actors, public speakers, and trial lawyers, develop the performance skills they need to win over an audience. I hope **Dynamic Song Performance** – A Singer's Bible will help you or your students accomplish your dreams.

Please utilize the Notes pages and make **Dynamic Song Performance** your own!

Pepper Jay

Overview

Whether you are a karaoke singer, an American Idol contestant, or a professional singer, there is always room for improvement. Enjoy your craft.

Dynamic Song Performance Method

The ***Dynamic Song Performance*** method begins by reinforcing successful performance skills while redirecting unsuccessful ones. The way performers think about themselves determines how much of their potential will develop and improve and how successfully they will navigate the artistic world of entertainment.

Dynamic Song Performance encompasses skill, confidence, and an attitude of believability. It is the ability to capture your audience and draw them into your story or remind them of one of their own. It is successfully transcending the lyrics into an emotional experience.

Dynamic Song Performance is a guide to the fundamentals of song performance. Included are encouraging, user-friendly song performance tips and exercises that are accessible to any performer. This text is for professional singers who want to increase mastery of song performance skills and arrive at or remain at the top of their craft. This book is also for singers at any phase of their career who crave more success and for aspiring singers who are considering going pro.

Dynamic Song Performance easily demonstrates comfortable and quickly improved technical, emotional, and psychological aspects of the craft of performance. It includes instruction on voice, sound, movement, space, confidence, and audience psychology.

Dynamic Song Performance helps singers find the performer within, overcome performance fears and open themselves up to their audience by developing a belief in their own creativity as a performer.

Dynamic Song Performance is the bridge that connects dreams to reality.

Pepper Jay
Photo by John Michael Ferrari

Chapter One.
General Information about Song Performance

What Is Song Performance?

What Are Song Performance Skills?

How Are Song Performance Skills Developed?

What Is a Song Performance Coach?

"Singing the correct notes does not a performance make." - Pepper Jay

Section 1A

What is Song Performance?

Believability Is the Key to Song Performance

Song Performance is the journey resulting in believability. A song is more than words. To be successful, a singing performance must convey believable words; a sincere connection between the song, the performance, and the artist. A true entertainer will transform a song into a total experience to be remembered and pleasantly recalled for a lifetime.

To achieve believability, song performance must include honest visual, auditory, and sensory output. It is an entire package that, together, results in honest sensual energy; sometimes referred to as "charisma."

Believability can transform a mediocre performance into genius and genius into amazing heights of creative inspiration and insight. Believability makes a singer look like a pro. In conjunction with the other song performance skills, a pro makes a performance look easy.

To arrive at true believability, you must find the performer within you without preconceptions. Own "it!" If you are overly self-conscious on stage or in a recording studio, perhaps you remain stuck in a state of emotional fear; afraid to make yourself vulnerable both to yourself and to your audience. Your willingness to share yourself with your audience is the first major step towards believability. The second step is training. Strengthening each of the song performance skills will take you closer to a believable song performance.

On this journey to believability, singers pass through imagination, creativity, and emotion.

An aside: One need only to listen to Billy Joel sing his first big hit song, "Piano Man" (1973), to appreciate magnificent song performance when one blends imagination, creativity, and emotion to successfully communicate a song.

Billy Joel - Photo courtesy of Associated Press

Imagination: So, you are not famous yet like Billy Joel? No worries. The first step is imagination. Imagine yourself already a star. Imagine yourself on a huge stage giving a wonderful performance. Visualize in your mind's eye every aspect of your performance. How will you look? How will you sound? How you will move? Now, imagine the faces of your audience as they gaze at you in adoration! Feel yourself smile as you realize your audience loves you! Smile at them. Imagine singing to them; singing for them. What you are doing is living your song performance first in your imagination.

By imagining your performance, you begin to build your performance and you begin to build confidence in yourself as a performer. In your imagination,

Side Note: Earl Nightingale's, "The Strangest Secret" (1956) remains the top-selling audio message in the personal development, self-help, and inspiration industry today. He would say, "You are what you think."

Thus, we begin with imagination. Find regular moments that allow you to close your eyes and visualize yourself as if you have already reached your singing and performance goals.

Creativity: Honing the freedom to be creative is essential for a great performance. Creativity makes your performance uniquely yours. Remember, that's where you want to arrive; at believability!

Think of your creativity as your own unique stamp on the things that you do. Turn your personality, quirks and all, into your personal creative performance stamp; your personal trademark. Lady Gaga did! So did Taylor Swift. They are two very different performers finding their own distinct path into our lives. What are your interesting characteristics?

Your audience needs to know who you are as a performer. Additionally, you need to know exactly who you are during your public performances, in the recording studio, and on film.

Please keep in mind that, when it comes to creativity, what might seem "over the top" in everyday life can be engaging and intriguing during a song. Be creative.

An aside: The singer-songwriter, multi-instrumentalist, and fashion designer, Gwen Stefani, is an excellent example of creativity and feeling comfortable in one's performance persona.

She is also a good example of a performer constantly changing but remaining true to who she is as a "brand" and as an artist.

Allow yourself special alone time to experiment with your style and performance. You cannot transform into the performer you want to be unless you try out new things to see what feels, looks, and sounds comfortable. Think out of the box. Exaggerate.

Record yourself getting big, loud, or silly. You might be surprised with the results. Share your creative experiments with others who completely support you in all you do.

An aside: Maybe it's the fashion designer in her, but Gwen Stefani's creativity in form and content adds inspiration to her amazing vibrato vocals.

Dynamic Song Performance

Gwen Stefani / No Doubt

Photo courtesy of Associated Press

Emotion: Actors and singers rarely spend time getting to know their true emotional selves. Sometimes it is easier to create an "on stage" emotional presence than it is to work on real life problems. When you are onstage or in front of a camera, your slightest glance and the smallest of gestures, even making eye contact with one audience member, can produce a tremendous emotional connection between you and your audience. That connection is one of believability and the result of excellent song performance. It is the result of you sharing your perceived emotion with

your audience. Sharing ... ahhhhhh!

Your emotional professional self during a performance should include two parts: First, convey to your audience that you are exactly where you want to be. Second, there is no one you would rather sing to than your current audience (and that includes your crew, background singers, musicians, camera operators, audio engineers, etc.).

Allison Iraheta – Photo by John Michael Ferrari

An aside: Allison Iraheta is an artist who doesn't worry about being like anyone else when it comes to her professional self. John Ferrari and I began coaching Allison just after she turned 12 years old and, even then, she knew she wanted to be rocker chic. Now, audiences continue to experience the evolution of Allison as a performer as she step-by-step grows and experiments with both her music and her looks. The photo, above, was shot a few months after Allison first started dying her hair red.

Dynamic Song Performance

I didn't think Allison changing her hair to red was a good idea. I was wrong. The red seems to have definitely added to the branding of the singing professional Allison Iraheta who, on occasion, tosses a strip of blue in her hair!

Allison Iraheta and Halo Circus (2013)

Section 1B

What Are Song Performance Skills?

Singers utilize and master different song performance skills depending on their goals and personality. In fact, song performance skills vary according to the proficiency of the performer. The following is a basic list of some of the skills all performers should keep in mind when they are on and off the stage and in the recording studio. I call it the Song Performance Skills Toolbox.

Song Performance Skills Toolbox:

Articulation and Diction	Audience Connection	Audience Psychology	Audition Skills
Believability	Body Movement	Emotional Exploration	Facial Expression
Grooming	Hand Movements	Individuality	Lyrical Expression
Microphone Technique	Movement	Musical Connection	Personality
Phrasing	Poise	Posture	Professionalism
Recording Techniques	Rhythm	Sensual Energy	Showmanship
Song Interpretation	Song Repertoire	Spatial Movement	Speaking Technique
Stage Humor	Style Development	Subtext	Timing
Vitality	Vocal Range	Voice Production	

Add to the Toolbox other song performance skills that you find helpful for you to remember to the empty boxes at the bottom Toolbox chart.

Circle each of the above song performance tools you want to improve. At every level of your development, re-visit the Song Performance Skills Toolbox to update your goals. Make a copy of this page or make a list of your song performance goals and post your list as a helpful reminder.

Understanding and perfecting the tools in your Song Performance Toolbox allows you to tap into the creative spirit inside yourself, the performer. Awaken those artistic feelings, thoughts, and emotions that result in confidence. The numerous rewards include a sense of freedom of expression and a greater appreciation for one's own talents. Your songs will "come to life" as beautiful believable expressions of communication. This should put a smile on your face and dollars in your pocket.

With your Song Performance Skills Toolbox available, watch successful performers like Bono and decide which of the performance tools they utilize. You will find that the most successful performers, like Lady Gaga, Snoop Lion aka Snoop Dog, Beyonce, or Madonna, have perfected most, if not all, of the Dynamic Song Performance Skills.

An aside: Bono, the Irish singer and musician, best known as the lead vocalist in the rock band U2, easily conveys confidence, joy, and freedom of expression to his audience. When Bono performs, he commands the stage. We know Bono loves to perform. We feel there's no place Bono would rather be than on stage entertaining us and there's no one he'd rather be performing for than the audience in front of him!

Bono / U2 – Photo courtesy of Associated Press

Section 1C

How Are Song Performance Skills Developed?

Use your Song Performance Skills Toolbox to start to identify your strengths and weaknesses for each performance skill. As you improve, your weaknesses will become your strengths. To develop and improve upon song performance skills, we must hone those techniques through countless rehearsals. The adage 'practice makes perfect' is true. Performers improve the more they rehearse. The irony is that we learn to "be in the moment" by practicing. Work hard, enjoy the process and learn the basic skills that will bring out the best performer in you.

Learn Your Craft. Like anything else worth learning, song performance skills take practice. Practice often. Put in the time and effort necessary not just to be good, but to be excellent ... wow them! I suggest a regular schedule or routine; a special time for you and your craft. Yes, anyone can get up at a party and sing some lyrics, but very few can truly entertain ... include yourself among the few! Learn your craft.

Explore Your Inner Universe. You are capable of becoming a better performer than you ever imagined. Let loose from the person you are and transform yourself into you, the entertainer. Remember, what is appropriate and expected of you on stage as a performer would probably get you fired from a "real life" day job. Who are you when you step on stage? What is your performer persona? These are questions that require specific answers.

What makes an audience want to return to see you perform over and over again? Certainly not the person you are at work as a waitress, lawyer, or taxi driver. No. Audiences become loyal fans because
the performer from your inner universe excites them and frees them from their own everyday persona.

Whether your style is smooth or animalistic, shake your audience up to change them for the better. Each time you successfully take your audience on an entertaining voyage, you have shared your inner performance universe with them. What joy to watch, listen, and experience your audience appreciate your singing performance!

Dynamic Song Performance

Garth Brooks – Photo courtesy of Associated Press

An aside: Garth Brooks is a perfect example of a singer who doesn't have to jump all over the stage in order to take his audience on an entertaining
journey.

Choose a performance style that is comfortable for you. After all, once your style is established and branded, you, the artist, will probably have to live with your chosen style throughout your career unless your style is to constantly change it; ala Madonna or Lady Gaga or Elton John.

Enjoy the Process! Performance skills are best developed through mutual respect between artist and coach and between artist and audience. Add to this mix, lots of laughter and good old-fashioned hard work, the result is the joy of performing.

Prince (RIP) – photo courtesy of Associated Press

It is easier to learn quickly if you are enjoying the learning process. How many singers get lost waiting for their "big break?" They wait to "be happy" until they have reached their goals; which usually include big money and fame, or winning a singing competition. These goals always seem to evade them, as does their happiness. Have you noticed that success usually comes to happy people? Would you rather share space with a happy person or one who is sad? Coincidence? I think not.

Clearly, the singer known as Prince enjoyed his craft. No matter how dramatic or upbeat his performance, Prince was one hundred percent committed to his performance for both his and our enjoyment.

Enjoy your craft ... enjoy the singing, the learning, the rehearsing, and, most of all, enjoy your audience. Your genuine smile is contagious ... spread it!

Dynamic Song Performance

Laura Martin – Cover Album
Photo by John Michael Ferrari

An aside: The singer guitarist Laura Martin is a presence to behold on stage. She really enjoys her craft; singing, playing guitar, and entertaining. Laura, who has exceptional range and variety in her vocal qualities, has a joy of life, which leads her to success on and off the stage.

Take Note: Never stop learning or rehearsing!! The mistake I see most often is the artist that feels they have "made it." They mistakenly think they no longer need to rehearse. They think that, because they have won a contest, signed with an agent, obtained a recording deal, or contracted for a tour, they no longer need to improve their skills. Accomplishments should be enjoyed as short-term goals, only. Nothing takes the place of continued learning and growing as an artist.

Section 1D

What is a Song Performance Coach?

The function of a song performance coach is to help the singer excel at each of the performance skills in the toolbox. The goal of a performance coach should be immediate results.

As the direct link between the singer's goals and success, the performance coach works closely on the voice as one of the performance tools but usually refers the client to a voice teacher when basic voiced

Simon Cowell on "American Idol" often said, "It's a singing competition." There seems to be a lack of importance placed on performance and performance coaches. This is not to diminish vocal coaches, who are essential, but as "American Idol," the "X Factor," "The Voice," "Duets," and "Opening Act" have taught us, the winners and runners-up aren't always the best singers but rather the artists
who are the most believable and best connect with the audience.

The song performance coach should assist artists in overcoming easily correctable vocal problems as they are encountered, such as faulty breathing and voice placement; dissolving the "break" to obtain vocal fluidity, and quickly and easily improving singing range.

Song performance coaches utilize vocal exercises as "homework" but sparingly take up coaching sessions singing scales or other vocal exercises. (Why spend money singing scales with a teacher when you can practice this at home?) The performance coach helps the artist become aware of vocal qualities and how to balance and manipulate them.

A coach should train the singer for successful singing and acting/singing auditions and for professional interviews and for recording sessions. An experienced performance coach, in conjunction with the artist's management, should be able to provide the talented artist with all of the tools to become a star.

An aside: Some, like the multi-talented Danika Quinn, make excellent song performance seem easy; like water running off of a duck's back. Danika is a perfect example of one classically trained but comfortable singing almost any place where nice people are listening, from a Vegas showroom to her Tinsel on the Town show.

How does a performance coach differ from a vocal teacher? A vocal teacher focuses almost exclusively on the voice without teaching onstage or recording skills. A vocal teacher should provide a working knowledge of your voice and how to use it. A vocal teacher ought to be able to teach a student about pitch, head and chest registers, volume control, sounds (vowels and consonants), vocal quality, and how to breathe properly. The vocal exercises utilized by singing teachers should help the student become aware of those qualities.

There are literally hundreds of voice teachers but only a handful of skilled performance coaches. Learn singing basics with the help of a singing teacher. If you desire heavy emphasis on vocal exercises and do not have the self-discipline to practice with a DVD, there are usually numerous voice teachers in every major city who specialize in improving voice through scales and other vocal exercises.

Once you have the basics, develop the performance tools to be the best singer you can be from a positive and nurturing song performance coach! Don't allow a supposed singing coach to disrespect you. Don't settle. Mediocrity is an artist who is satisfied with just memorizing words and singing, hopefully, on key. Your singing profession can be more satisfying than "good." Find a performance coach that fits well with you and your goals and learn to be "great!" Awesome!

Carefully choose both singing teachers and a song performance coach who love teaching. The next best thing to performing is for a coach to experience talented singers, actors, and musicians while guiding them through informative and fun journeys toward their professional goals. Choose a voice teacher or a song performance coach in which you have confidence. If your confidence is well placed, you will develop a long-term trusting relationship with professionals who will effectively assist you during your performance career. This is especially true when well intentioned or not-so-well-intentioned recording companies and professional management try to take over your career.

Pepper Jay and Danika Quinn
Photo by John Michael Ferrari

Tips on How to choose a voice teacher or performance coach. Take note:

1. Often singers who have not "made it" in their own careers become "voice teachers."

2. When choosing a voice teacher, try to select one from a recommendation or referral instead of from the teacher's website or the Yellow Pages.

3. Audition your voice teacher or performance coach. Speak with them about your goals and how they can help you achieve them.

4. Make sure you're getting the real teacher and not the assistant.

5. Will the teacher or coach allow you to videotape or record all or part of your coaching sessions?

6. Will the teacher take up most of the lesson time with scales or other exercises you can do at home on your own dime?

7. Ask to speak to past students of the professional you are considering

to hire.

8. Don't sign any long-term contracts with a teacher or coach. I like the 90-day rule. Have they significantly helped improve the singing and/or singing performance during the last 90 days? If not, find another teacher or coach.

9. Most importantly, do you like the teacher or coach? Are they someone with whom you'd like to have a long-term professional relationship?

Cautionary Note: Every major city has singing or performance schools. These schools are a good start for the amateur and can be fun, particularly for young singers, but a professional or a would-be professional requires more personal attention.

Subtle distinction when choosing the best performance coach for you: Try not to rely on those who create performers or entertainers from a formula. Rather, seek guidance from a coach or teacher who will pull the performer and entertainer out of you. If you, the performer, are packaged using what comes naturally to you, your audiences will accept you more easily ... the public will better accept you as believable.

Chapter Two.
How to Do IT!

Audience Psychology Is EVERYTHING!

The Importance of an INTRA-Audience Bond of Appreciation

Be Sincere with Your Lyrics Be Sincere with Your Patter Will Them To look at You

The Cameras are Some of Your Audience Members Your audience is your friend.

"It is your audience you are entertaining ... you are not just solo singing in the shower!" - Pepper Jay

Section 2A
Audience Psychology is EVERYTHING!

As a song performer, audiences are your greatest allies. It is essential that you establish basic audience psychology performance skills to better connect with them. With practiced skills, you and your audience will form a mutually beneficial relationship regardless of the size or type of audience or the day of your performance. However, for live performances, it always helps to know as much as possible about your audience and to be aware of the day of the week you will be performing.

Audiences have many different moods. They can be happy, fickle, capricious, steadfast, relaxed, uptight, energetic, high, anxious, insensitive, or sleepy; just to name a few. However, all audiences have one thing in common: They all want to be entertained and secretly hope you can fulfill the job. Each type of audience will present you with a unique challenge, but few audiences, if any, are bad. To the best of your ability, try to figure out the reason your audience exists. For example, will your audience be the kind who wants to dance in their seats? Sing along with you? Carry signs with your name on it?

Some believe the day of the week has a large impact on the psychology of an audience. I've heard it said that on Tuesdays, audiences are usually thought to be quiet. Since Wednesday is the "hump" day of the week, people tend to be a little more relaxed. Thursdays may bring in a rowdier crowd. Of course, on Friday, audiences are more relaxed albeit somewhat tired, it being the beginning of the weekend. And Saturday night will provide you with the most solid and lively audience experience. In addition, matinees or afternoon audiences usually consist of the very young and/or the very old.

The audience psychology skills in this text may be successfully applied to any type of audience; young, teens, Millennials, Generation X, Baby Boomers, or the elderly. Once audience psychology skills are effectively used, they "wow" audiences of every musical genre; rap, country, jazz, rock n roll, religious, hip hop, reggae, folk, heavy metal, or pop.

The venues that experienced Thurston Watts on stage truly appreciated his great song performance. First, there was Thurston's talented voice. Then, there was the realization that Thurston never had a stranger in his audience. You can still find some clips of Thurston's performances on the Internet. When you watch Thurston perform, notice how he directs his attention to individual audience members in such a way that everyone feels included. More information about Thurston, who was one of the lead singers in the oldies band, "Ferrari & Friends," from 1993 to his death in 2009, may be found at www.ThurstonWatts.com.

Thurston Watts (RIP)
Photo by Pepper Jay

As a teen opera singer, Golda Berkman sings almost exclusively to large audiences made up of adults. Golda uses the song performance skills in this text to connect with her audience as if they were her best friends.

Pepper Jay and Golda Berkman 2014
Photo by John Michael Ferrari

The focus of audience psychology is not on the audience. The focus of audience psychology is on you, the artist, and on your performance attitude toward your audience. What follows are basic audience psychology skills to be utilized in your own unique way. Welcome to the world of audience psychology!

No One Is a Stranger
Key: There are no strangers in your audience! Believe that every audience member is your friend. Walk out onto that stage or into the recording studio prepared to greet your best friends. Your audience wants to like you and be entertained by your singing performance. Be real. Enjoy what you do. Enjoy your audience. Your appreciative state of mind is everything.

Your audience may have assembled for numerous reasons: to listen, to dance, to meet people, to appreciate, to wind down, to gear up, whatever. No matter why your audience was created, your goal remains the same: you want your audience to enjoy you, the performer, as you mutually enjoy them, your audience.

Name Your Chair
The stage or recording studio also need not be a stranger, even if you've never been there before. First, name your chair. My chair, no matter where I am, is Harvey. I wonder what Harvey is going to look like or feel like in new situations such as auditions, interviews, meetings, or just sitting on Harvey on a stage. But, one thing I do know for sure, Harvey is MY chair. He belongs to me. I treat Harvey like he is mine. I touch him. Feel the length of my back against him. Wherever I am, in any location, if there is a chair there for me to sit on, he's my Harvey.

Own the Floor
No chair or stool or couch? Own the floor and the space around you. I will be chatting later in this text about feeling the floor beneath you with four parts of the bottom of your feet, bending knees to push and "own" the stage beneath them. With this state of mind, no one, not person nor object, is a stranger. Audience and crew are your good friends and you own the theater or recording studio! You belong there.

If you are confident that you belong on stage, then that confidence will transfer over to your audience. This mutual confidence is the first major step in the best use of audience psychology.

Section 2B
The Importance of an INTRA-Audience Bond of Appreciation

Key: It's you and them. The moment someone becomes a "member" of an audience, no matter how large or small the venue, the potential for an invisible "audience bond" is created. This audience bond is separate and different from your bond with your audience. Instead, this is an intra-audience bond; you want your audience to bond with itself!

Your ultimate goal using this performance tool is to create, transform, nurture, and strengthen that potential intra-audience bond into reality. When successful, the resulting audience bond is palpable. The audience shares anticipation, joy, and appreciation. What a dream come true to be the center catalyst of the entire audience's joined appreciation!

Once your audience members bond with each other, you can more successfully forge a mutual bond of appreciation with the entire audience as one spirit. In order to create an inter-audience bond, you first must facilitate the intra-audience bond. Once established, whether yours is an audience of 10 or 10,000, the inter-audience bond you form with your audience is real and lasting.

Your job as the entertainer is to help your audience transcend their current emotional state to something higher; something better. People look to entertainment for different reasons but, as we all know, one of the prevalent reasons is to escape our daily anxieties and get lost, albeit for a moment, in another less-stressed world. Give your audience the gift of bonding with itself and then with you.

Personal Attention is the Key to Inter-Audience Bonding.

When you give one audience member positive & complete personal attention it can result in a gift to your entire audience. Personal attention given to an audience member is the most important audience psychology technique because it is the least understood by most schools, coaches, and teachers.

Each time you focus on one audience member and then another and another, the entire audience experiences not only your individual attention, but also the anticipation that they may be next on your

personal attention list! Even though each and every audience member may be interpreting your performance differently, consciously or unconsciously, each appreciates the attention. It's you and them. If you connect with one audience member, you begin to connect with them all!

When you smile or nod at someone on the street, what is their natural reaction? Correct! That stranger will usually smile or nod back at you in return. An audience is no different. Be generous with your smiles and nods of appreciation with your audience.

Your goal is to transform your audience into a mutual bond of anticipation, enjoyment, and appreciation. An inter-audience bonding is created; just you and them. How joyful when an audience appreciates your talents.

Kenyatta Mackey
Photo by John Michael Ferrari

An aside: Kenyatta Mackey, who tours all over the world with her "Baby Dolls," knows how to bring lyrics to life. Kenyatta, who can sing in five languages, has the ability to take her audience on unique journeys.

Section 2C
Be Sincere With Your Lyrics

Key: Make your song and patter real.
Communicate the song as if you mean the words - as if you are sharing a special communication only with your audience. Sing as if your audience is the "target" of the song. Depending upon the lyrics, the target might be your best friend, lover, ex-boyfriend or girlfriend, mother, rival, etc.

Make the song personal.
Key: Express the lyrics as you would in conversation. Share the lyrics as if you are making the words up "on the spot," like you do when you're not following a script. In "real life," we don't always know what we're going to say before we say it. A more advanced song performance skill is to try to phrase your lyrics as if you were thinking them up at the moment. Keep it subtle and simple. You are correct to think that this performance skill is usually easier when singing with "live" musicians, but it can also be accomplished when singing to "tracks". When successful, you transform your performance into a more meaningful experience.

Create an attitude appropriate to the song. Bring the song alive. Make the song yours. Feel the song and the importance, or unimportance,. of your communication of the music and lyrics. Enjoy your "unique"

sharing of your song with your audience. Whether your performance is live or recorded, your enjoyment and appreciation of the lyrics and music is the kernel that defines you as an entertainer; as a star.

Think, Internalize, Share: the Make it Look Real Exercise:

Think: Think about the lyrics before you sing them. This can be easily accomplished during the introduction of the song and during an instrumental. But, with practice, it can be quickly accomplished during the briefest of instrumental pauses. When you think about the words, your face reflects those thoughts and the audience receives a "preview" of what is to come.

Many acting coaches refer to this as "subtext," the underlying meaning or message of the lyric. I like to refer to it as an unspoken thought. For example, when Fantasia sang the classic "Summertime" during her winning performances on "American Idol, Season Three," she brought to the song a sensitive subtext of the trials and tribulations of a young black female in America. As Fantasia thinks about the lyrics just prior to singing them, we can see her struggle and her pain. The Internet is a great way to view and learn from great performers.

Internalize: Give yourself a second or two to ponder on the meaning of the lyrics. For example, Willie Nelson's lyrics, "Crazy, I'm crazy for feeling so lonely ..." could invoke a variety of thoughts.

When Patsy Cline sings "Crazy," we can feel the yearning in her voice.

As the singer, you make the song your own by choosing how you are going to internalize those lyrics; loneliness, foolishness, sadness, vulnerability, etc. As you take that second or two to internalize the lyrics, your face and your entire body will begin to communicate that internalization to your audience.

Share: Finally, after you have prepared your audience with thought and meaning, you perform the lyrics for your audience. The lyrics will not come as a surprise. Your audience knew what was coming because you gave them your thinking and internalization as extra gifts. The sharing of your song does not begin with the first lyric. It begins with your thoughts and your self – internalization of your thoughts. Share with your audience so that your audience becomes the 2nd half of your lyrical conversation.

Speak The Words Exercise: Practice speaking the lyrics instead of singing the lyrics. What is the meaning of each lyrical phrase? How would that phrase sound if you were saying those words in a real conversation? For purposes of this exercise, be careful not to speak the lyrics to the rhythm of the melody. Forget the song completely. No singing, no humming, just speak the words as if they are lines in a script and you are the actor. Make your audience believe your acting performance is realistic. Express the words as if they are yours. Record yourself doing this exercise and listen and watch how you deliver the spoken words. The trick is to keep this sense of reality when you return to singing the song!

Speak The Words Differently Exercise: Practice speaking the lyrics as a different person or with a different accent. For example, if you are 22 years old, speak the words as an 80 year old, as a 5 year old, as a minister, as a gang member. If you are from the north, speak the lyrics as if you were from the south. The variations on this exercise are endless. Listen to yourself. Watch yourself. Experience how the lyrics come alive when spoken for the first time. Record yourself rehearsing performance skills whenever possible!

Strong Enunciation Exercise: Speak the words with strong enunciation. Practice speaking the lyrics with over-exaggerated consonants. For example, over emphasize all of the d's, k's, p's, and t's (but don't pop them into the mic). A slightly toned down version of the extra enunciation of the consonants adds emotion to the word s. Enunciation helps the lyrics come alive!

Note: Singing a song "just like the record" might be good for cover bands or professional impersonators or tribute artists, but not such a good idea for those who want to carve their own niche in the music business. Make the song your own. Let the best "you" shine through and tell the story.

Section 2D
Be Sincere With Your Patter

Patter is the "chit chat" you make with your audience between songs and sometimes during musical introductions and instrumental breaks. Whether it is the thank you after applause and an introduction of the next song or a story about how you made minute rice last night, be truly interested in sharing the information with your audience. Trust your audience enough to share part of the personal you. Remember, your audience wants to be your friend!

As in "real life" communication, keep your "patter" interesting by using variations in pitch and tonality. Pitch changes prevent patter from becoming monotone. Your patter with your audience will continue to be interesting if you use higher and lower pitches as you express your ideas.

The use of pitch changes in your patter also helps communicate your state of mind. High and varied tones usually represent elation of spirit and excitement. Low and uniform tones can represent depression of spirit or a special confidence with others or an acceptance of others. Let your song dictate your state of mind.

If you are new to the concept of pitch changes, begin with the "step method." Divide your words into phrases and say each phrase beginning with a high pitched note and then lower your pitch for each remaining word in the phrase as if you were walking your voice down a flight of steps. As you practice, vary the pitch changes to add interest.

People lift their limbs, their bodies and their minds when they start to do something. When they complete what they have to do, people let their hands fall at their sides or they lie down or sit down. Our lungs rise with inspiration of breath and fall with expiration of breath. These seem to be laws of nature. Thus, the upward or downward use of pitch not only expresses your motivation but also keeps your patter new, appealing, alive, and meaningful.

Danika Quinn
Photo by John Wright

An aside: Yes, Danika Quinn is beautiful but that's not the only reason her singing performances remain appealing and alive. Danika designs song performance with her beautiful temptress vocals as well as her expressive body, her use of breath, and her addictively comic personality. When Danika sings to you, she performs with sincerity. You really believe what Danika is saying and you know, for sure, she is communicating directly with you!

Section 2E
Will Them to Look At You

Key: Look Into Their Eyes.
Pretend you have extraordinary powers and can make each audience member look at you. Always look right into their eyes or where their eyes should be. Often, you can't see the eyes of each audience member. Sometimes the lights are too bright or an audience member is turned away. If you can't see the "whites of their eyes," look at them as if you could. Interestingly enough, if you look at the back of someone's head as if they are looking right back at you, the vast remainder of your audience will not know the difference. On the other hand, your audience will pick up every uncomfortable nuance if you're searching or pleading for someone to return your gaze.

Sing with the actual or pretend knowledge, realization, and satisfaction that your audience can't take their eyes off of you. That satisfaction and confidence, alone, will take you one step closer to greatly improved song performance skills.

Don't Abandon Your Audience
Key: Give each audience member a complete lyrical phrase.
Some of the most helpful song performance tools are those that prevent audience abandonment. This is particularly true because these tools are rarely understood by teachers or coaches. What is audience abandonment? If someone looks at you and begins the sentence, "I love ..." and then looks away before saying "you" the result is that you feel abandoned. You are not convinced that it is <u>you</u> who is loved.
Keep your attention on one audience member or on one audience section when your venue is huge, for the entire length of the phrase of the song. Do not change your focus from one member to another in the middle of a phrase. Give each audience member, or audience section, the gift of an entire phrase to be remembered.

Lyrical Phrases
What is a lyrical phrase? For purposes of Dynamic Song Performance, it is a complete thought. Enough of a thought that, along with the performance of that thought, your audience member won't feel cheated after you look away.

Depending upon the lyrics, your lyrical phrase can be as short as one word or a prepositional phrase or as long as a complete sentence.
Do your grammar lessons come to mind? Some examples of lyrical phrases are: "I can't waste time," "I used to rule the world," "it's too soon to see," "in time," and "from my heart."

Remember, a lyrical phrase is not necessarily a complete sentence but it must be a complete thought.

How often you interact with one audience member may be influenced by the genre of song you are singing. If your song is one that would be found on young hip channels such as MTV or FUSE, the lyrical phrase may come fast and furious, like the cuts of an MTV video. Perhaps, even as short as one word. If, however, your song belongs more on VH-1 or other "middle of the road" pop channels, your lyrical phrases may be longer. Thus, your individual attention to one audience member or audience section will be longer, perhaps as long as a prepositional phrase, such as, "into the valley." However, if your song is a ballad or has a more country flavor, as are songs found on CMT or other country channels, you might stay with one audience member or audience section for an entire sentence.

An aside: Whether Luisa LuBell is singing in English or in Spanish, in musical theatre or on a pop concert stage, she performs as if she belongs to her audience.

Luisa LuBell - Photo by John Wright

Experience Your Audience
Key: Only Close Your Eyes For A Reason and Only For A Moment.
Probably the most frustrating experiences for an audience occur when a singer consistently sings with closed eyes. At first, the audience may be intrigued. But, soon, the only person entertained is the singer. The audience is no longer a player but rather is sidelined, limited to the position of voyeur, uncomfortably attempting to be interested in the singer's internal performance. Audiences don't usually pay money to watch a singer. Audience members purchase a ticket in an attempt to enjoy completely connecting with the entertainer; visually, auditorily, and kinetically.

On the other hand, your clever use of closing your eyes at the perfect moments in the song can be extremely effective, such as during a momentary instrumental break or when the lyrics lend themselves to internal introspections.

Come Back To Me
Key: Time the Closing and Opening of Your Eyes Carefully.
Closing your eyes during a song can heighten the song's emotional performance. The basic rule I created about closing your eyes is always return to the same audience member or section you were looking at prior to your eyes closing.

For example, as you look at the lady in the 3rd row the lyrics begin, "I just don't know," the song pauses with an instrumental lick as you slightly lower and turn your head to the side and close your eyes to meditate on what you have to say, turn your head back, then, and only then, reopen your eyes looking at the same lady in the 3rd row, and finish the lyrical sentence, "when I'll see you again."

If, after closing your eyes, you return to look at the man in the next row, not only will your 3rd row lady feel abandoned but the entire live and camera audience may experience a disconnect and never understand the reason why. This is an important audience psychology concept.

Don't Sing to Yourself
Key: Sing to and for your audience.
An audience doesn't last very long when singers continually sing only to themselves. With few exceptions, even if the singer is really enjoying his own performance, an audience will eventually lose interest as voyeur. Your eyes must do overtime as you are singing.

The Three Step Punch, described in more detail later in this text, explains more fully this special audience relationship technique.

In summary:

Step One, your eyes tell your audience that there is no other place you would rather be and you are glad you are with them.

Step Two, your eyes tell your audience that you appreciate they are with you. Your eyes make the main connection with your audience ... you want to see "eye to eye" with your audience in more ways than one. Your eyes help you communicate your song.

And, Step Three, your eyes assure your audience members that, although you have to leave them for a moment, you will return to them.

Section 2F
The Camera is One of Your Audience Members

Key: Don't look for the camera, let the camera find you.
There is nothing more unprofessional than to realize a singer, or anyone on stage, is searching for the camera. Let the cameras find you. Much of the best footage of your performance is shot from the side where the microphone is not blocking your mouth. As you focus intently on one audience member or one audience section, the camera audience will also experience that special connection.

When you are "on camera," include each of the cameras as if they are an audience member. Apply all of your audience psychology techniques to each camera as that camera comes naturally within your range of vision. Remember, the camera is active when it has a red light on (usually on top). When a camera is near you, play to that camera as if it is an audience member whether or not the red light of the camera is on!

Zigzag Method
Key: Don't avoid sections of your audience.
Use my zigzag method when your attention is traveling from one audience member to another. For example, if you are singing to the left loge section of your audience and then you turn your attention to the right loge section, (see chart below) the result will be that the center section that you skipped over will feel cheated or abandoned. Instead, go from the left loge to the mezzanine center and then perhaps

up to the balcony center and then down to the mezzanine right and finally down to the lower right loge. Your attention has zigzagged through the audience without obviously skipping over any particular section.

Balcony Left	Balcony Center	Balcony Right
Mezzanine Left	Mezzanine Center	Mezzanine Right
Loge Left	Loge Center	Loge Right

Audience Sections

The zigzag method is also effective when working a single section of a large audience or smaller audience. Begin in the center and then zigzag your attention without skipping over several audience members. The following audience member chart will demonstrate.

Each rectangle is an audience member.. Each # is a lyrical phrase in your song. Always try to begin and end an important phrase, in the center mezzanine section, or to or near the center audience members.

			#4	
	#8	#5		#3
#7		#1		
	#6		#2	

Sample zig-zag Audience pattern

Stimulate From All Sides
Key: Stimulate your audiences' senses with "information intake" words.

Audience members take in information in different ways. Some audience members are more visual and understand better when they are shown something new; they "picture" the idea. Other audience members are more auditory and they therefore depend on their listening skills to retrieve information; to them it's "loud and clear." And still other audience members "feel" or "sense" what is being communicated. Kinetically becoming aware of their surroundings; they "get it!" You, as the entertainer, should communicate to all 3 types in your audience. Your singing and patter performance skills include all of you; vocal, physical, mental, and emotional. It's not just what you sing but how you sing it and how you feel about sharing with your audience.

Thus, not only should your singing performance stimulate several senses, your "patter" should also cover the bases in order to stimulate your audiences' senses. "Patter," in this context, refers to what you say to your audience or to your performance partner(s), before or after the song or during the song but outside of the song's lyrics, such as during the musical introduction.

Sprinkle different "sense" words throughout your patter; mixing and matching to "connect" with as many of your audience members as possible. For example, "I see" what you mean (for the visual audience members). And, "I hear" what you're saying (for the auditory audience members). Add phrases such as "I feel" or "I understand" or "I sense" for the touchy feely kinetic members of your audience.

An aside: When it comes to sharing feelings on stage, the sensual songstress, Rebecca Kyler Downs, has a corner on the market. It's a wonder that her microphone doesn't melt every time Rebecca sings a lyrical phrase or shoots one of her many intimate looks to her audience.

How Do I Take In Information Exercise: Pay attention to the word phrases you use. Jot them down as you hear yourself saying them. Record yourself. Your choice of words determines how you take in information. What kind of words do you use most? Are they verbal words, sound words, or physical words? Once you determine how you take in information, write out other sense words that you could use that would better communicate with those who take in information differently. Whether it's an audience of a thousand or a business meeting of a dozen, it's a good idea to include all three kinds of "information in-take" words in your "patter" or discussion with your audience.

More "Stimulate from all Sides" Examples:

Visual: And, then, I caught sight of ...; I see what you mean ...; it's clear to me ...

Auditory: I listen to ...; sounds like ...; we should work in harmony with ...

Kinetic: I get the impression that ...; the bottom line
is ...; I wasn't aware that ...; I feel that ...

Note: Please see the reference to author and life instructor Anthony Robbins in attached Bibliography. I try to incorporate what I learn from the teachings of Mr. Robbins into my audience psychology performance skills as well as in my daily life.

Serious Subjects Key: Keep it neutral.
No politics or religion ... nothing serious! Unless the purpose of your performance is to sway opinion or to promote a cause, or to be a political comedy singer, keep the subject matter of your performance "neutral." Be careful to avoid commenting on subjects that alienate part of your audience. Generally, your audience has bonded for a purpose: to be entertained. If your audience wanted to be educated, they would probably have attended a night class, a lecture, or a political rally instead of a nightclub or concert!

If you want to teach your audience, teach by example. Be polite, respectful, gracious, understanding, sharing, professional, and appreciative. Even good performers of genres like rock, rap, and punk are usually respectful to their audience.

The Three-Step Punch
Key: Build well rounded and complete audience relationships.
The Three Step Punch, briefly referred to earlier, specifically breaks down the "how to" of your communication with an audience member.

The Three-Step Punch, Step One: I'm glad you're here.
You're glad to be where you are performing. And, as you look directly into

the eyes of one of your audience members, think to yourself, "I'm glad you're here tonight, too!" Your entire audience will

be moved by your glance. You should do what comes to you naturally in order for you to communicate your joy at finding that person in your audience. Step one could be a twinkle of the eye, a nod of the head, a wink, a slight grin, special smile, a shoulder or chin move, and/or make up your own combinations. But, believe it for real and make it real. This is not a make-believe relationship. Your relationships with your audiences should be moments to remember forever. Step One is your chance to show your appreciation; an opportunity to share you and your music and song with your audience member.

Celine Dion is an excellent example of a singer who has an honest and believable relationship with her audience. Apart from her technically skilled and powerful vocals, Celine Dion sings directly to and for her audience. Watch Celine Dion as her attention never strays from her vocal and visual gifts. Take a moment to observe Celine's audience members so that you may witness how convinced they are that Celine Dion is glad that each and every audience member is part of her performance.

Dynamic Song Performance

Celine Dion / Photo courtesy of Associated Press

If you find Step One difficult without looking fake, do not despair. Study yourself to discover how you genuinely react when you are introduced to someone you like. Sing to yourself in the mirror. Or, record yourself singing to a camera. Once you begin to understand your own reactions, practice re-creating those feelings and reactions when glancing at an audience member or audience section.

Study Yourself Exercise: Video tape yourself pretending to meet someone you know you are attracted to (this can be someone you know or a movie star you'd like to meet, etc). With the camera on "record," turn your back to the camera and take the time to picture in your mind the person you will soon see. What will they look like? How will they sound? How will they make you feel? Turn around and see the person in the camera and, without speaking, take 15 seconds to enjoy that person. Stop the camera and re-watch yourself. If you take this exercise seriously, you will notice the pleasure in your eyes. Did your eyes twinkle? Did your head move up and down or tilt to the side? What did your mouth look like, did you break out in a big grin or did your smile slowly increase with appreciation? What you see on camera is the beginning of your Step One!

The Three-Step Punch, Step Two: Lyrics, the complete phrase
Give your audience member the gift of a lyrical phrase; at least an entire phrase of the lyrics to one audience member or to one audience section. Communicate the lyrical phrase using your song performance skills as if you were just thinking the words up ... as if you were communicating in a real conversation or argument or plea, depending on the subject matter of the song. This may be the most important song performance skill one may develop!

Unless the song is dedicated to a particular audience member (i.e., in honor of your anniversary, etc), do not sing more than an entire sentence of the lyrics to any one audience member or audience section. If you do, the remainder of your audience will feel abandoned.

The Three-Step Punch, Step Three: I'll be back. When you have finished singing the lyrical phrase, but before leaving your audience member or section, let them know that you will be back. Think to yourself, "I'll see you later" or "I'll be back" or "Thank you." Step Three is a special movement that accompanies the thought such as in Step One. This might be a special look, a grin, and any recognition of respect from you to your audience member or audience section that will make them feel special.

You may be used to spending so much time looking into the eyes of someone you don't know. But, don't rush from your audience member. It takes less than a ½ a second to confirm your relationship in Step Three.

One way to practice Step Three is to delay your eyes from leaving your first audience member as your nose begins to seek out your second audience member. The delay can be as quick as a ¼ of a second. This slight delay will give the impression of your reluctance in leaving your first audience member. Practice this subtle move until it looks natural and not contrived. Nose, eyes, look and repeat.

Three Step Punch Exercise
Set up a camera to record yourself in front of a pretend audience. Create your pretend audience members using stuffed animals, magazine photos, dolls, drawings, whatever. Record yourself singing while giving the Three Step Punch to each of your audience members. Repeat as necessary until your relationship with your audience members are enjoyable, easy and convincing.

Chapter Three.
A Little Structure Helps Communicate Your Song

Phrasing Enunciation

Build the Song

Vocal Performance Tips

Body Movement – Compliment the Phrasing

It's All in Your Eyes and Facial Expressions

"Learn the details of song performance skills, but don't get caught up in the details." - Pepper Jay

Section 3A
Phrasing

Key: Make love not war.
I refer to three types of phrasing in songs – lyrical, musical, and the relationship of the lyrics to the music. "Phrasing" is often lyrically defined as "a sequence of words intended to have meaning. Its musical definition is often a short passage or segment, often consisting of four measures or forming part of a larger unit.

In this text, I focus mainly on the third type of musical phrasing; the relationship of the placement of the lyric to the musical note.

The song performance goal is to design the lyrics and the music to "make love;" allowing each to be appreciated on its own while, at the same time, introducing, accenting, or harmonizing with the other. In contrast, are lyrics and music that "make war" with each other and compete for their sounds or emphasis to take place at the same moment.

Excellent phrasing can make a good singer/entertainer remembered for a lifetime. The perfect example of this is Frank Sinatra who became known for his "phrasing." Sinatra sang between the music, and is sometimes referred to as a "phraseologest." Sinatra rarely sang where he would be competing with the strings or the horns. Sinatra allowed the lyrics and the music to make love, not war.

"Frank Sinatra was the first, and arguably the last, great "song stylist." [He] came to inhabit and define the most elegant and sophisticated pop tunes ever written. ... once he had insinuated himself into a song, it was impossible to imagine it without him." Quoting from Rolling Stones Article, "One For the Road; Frank Sinatra sang out our soul," posted May 15, 1998, by MARK A. MEHLE

Make the song your own. Frank Sinatra's phrasing was different from most pop songs of the 50's, which were written for the lyric and the musical note, particularly the down beat, to share the same space. Sinatra's arrangers created musical arrangements that had room to breathe. Unless an arrangement is a wall of music, you should be able to find a place to express your lyrics without competing with a heavy musical note.

Does your placing of the lyrics make love or make war with your music? Polished phrasing that compliments the music is like a branch dancing lovingly with the breeze. In contrast, a heavy downbeat that competes with a lyric not only makes it difficult to hear and understand the lyrics, but it creates tension as if the lyrical branch wants to break in a musical storm.

Phrasing Exercise
Effective phrasing requires quality practice. If there is any absolute rule one must follow to have excellent phrasing, it is to sing while trying different ways to express the lyrics. As you force yourself to think of new ways to approach the same tune, you force yourself to sing something differently. That kind of pressure should result in you becoming a better singer, and allowing you to explore new and different phrasing you wouldn't normally have tried.

Make Love Not War With The Music Exercise: Choose a song with a strong downbeat and then practice "tailing the downbeat." In other words, instead of singing the lyric on the downbeat, practice singing the lyrical word after the downbeat or after the beginning of the downbeat so that your lyric becomes the downbeat's shadow or tail. Experiment, experiment, experiment!

Hint: Is there is a particular singer you admire for their phrasing ability? If yes, try to figure out what it is about their phrasing you like and then practice duplicating that admired technique. Once you have practiced their technique a zillion times, add a touch of your personality and create a phrasing style of your own. For those of you who sing previously published songs, remember that just because the original artist sang the lyrics crashing over the notes doesn't mean you must sing it with the same warlike phrasing. Try not to lose lyrics in the downbeat.

Dynamic Song Performance

Allison Iraheta and John Michael Ferrari
Photo by Pepper Jay

An aside: Don't give up. The first time I showed up with 12 year old Allison Iraheta at a country club for her to perform with the "oldies" band "Ferrari & Friends," the manager told me he didn't want a child on his stage. I said to him, "Let's make a deal. If, after Allison sings one song, you want her off the stage, then she's gone, otherwise, all is good." Allison sang the first verse of a song and the manager rushed over to me with a big smile on his face. "She's wonderful," he said. "You can bring Allison Iraheta to our stage anytime." And, I did. Allison Iraheta performed with the oldies group, "Ferrari & Friends," from 2004 when Allison was twelve, until 2008, when she became top four on "American Idol, Season 8."

Section 3B
Enunciation

Singing Enunciation Brings Passion to the Lyrics Singing Enunciation is the art of clearly and concisely pronouncing the lyrics as you sing. Excellent enunciation breathes your songs to life and conveys the lyrics' passion. Clever use of strong enunciation heightens every emotion; love, lust, sadness, anger. Enunciation gives "kick" to the lyrics. If there is any incorrect song performance technique that lowers a singer's chance of success it is the singer's lack of enunciation of the lyrics. Not so much fun when the listener cannot understand the lyrics of the song.

To achieve better singing enunciation, move your tongue and lips fully as you pronounce the lyrics. If you become careless in your enunciation, audiences will lose interest as your singing becomes difficult to understand or muffled into the music.

Most Common Singing Enunciation Errors
Watch out for the most common singing enunciation error: dropping off the end of words, particularly "ed," "d," "p," or "t." Note that it is not an error when singers knowingly change the "ing" at the end of a lyric to "in," for a softer sound without the "g," which can be an exceptionally good technique, especially for the softer country, romantic, or new age genres.

Unless you are performing musical comedy, a second common singing enunciation error is muffling the middle of words. This usually occurs accidentally by replacing sharper consonant sounds (like "t") with softer sounds (like "d"). The softer sounds require less muscle energy. However, when your lyric is "butter" but you sing it like "budder" your audience, either consciously or unconsciously, feels uncomfortable. Muffled lyrics create incongruent and unprofessional "out of whack" performances and sound less educated!

Practice Makes Articulate
Rid yourself of a singing enunciation problem (or sloppy singing) with diligent practice. Perhaps you have picked up poor speaking enunciation habits that could also use improving. No worries. Record yourself, listen to yourself, and demand perfect enunciation of yourself. It will take a lot of effort but, with practice, you should be able to articulate perfectly.

Dynamic Song Performance

Brandon James
Photo by John Michael Ferrari

An accomplished vocalist, guitarist, and lyricist, Brandon James embraces a variety of music genres from spiritual inspirations to country to pop to creation of his own unique country sound described as "west coast country." Originally from Canada, Brandon committed large segments of time to perfecting his singing enunciation skills which resulted in a delightful blend of a Canadian American pop-rock experience.

Over-Exaggeration Exercise: Practice both singing and speaking your lyrics with over-exaggerated consonants. Use "over the top" intense consonants, such as the "d's," "j's," "k's," "p's," and "t's." Open your mouth wide and make large mouth movements as you "spit" out the consonant sounds. Practice the song over and over again, retaining the stronger consonant sounds and slowly eliminating the exaggerated mouth and face changes. Professional singers often employ this as a warm-up exercise just prior to performing or recording.

Note: It is not an error when a singer intentionally "softens" a vowel sound in order to take the harshness out of a lyrical phrase. This is sometimes called "spreading the vowel." Actually, unless it's a comedy routine, a professional singer rarely sings with strong enunciation of vowels.

Al Boyd
Photo by John Wright

Al Boyd has enjoyed singing with the Imperial Wonders, the O'Jays, the Matadors, The

Temptations, and with Ferrari & Friends, to name a few. Regardless of the grouping, Al Boyd always brings high energy and a crisp enunciation of his consonants to deliver the true meaning of the lyrics regardless of the genre Al Boyd is performing.

Section 3C
Build the Song

Key: Take your audience on a journey.
Just as a story leads a reader on a journey from beginning to middle to end, your song should escort your audience on a similar journey. Each portion of your song should guide your audience to a higher or different level than the previous portion.

Your performance during the song's instrumental beginning or lead-in, no matter how short or long, should "introduce" the song's essence and give the audience a sample of your mood; a titillation of what is to follow. Usually, you will want to start your performance small and subtle so you have somewhere to build. Give your audience just a little more of something as each verse and bridge is performed. Think peaks and valleys.

When building the performance of your song, be aware of your song's "hook." The "hook" is that one line of lyric and music designed to "catch" the listener's ear, keep the listener's interest during the song, and leave the listener with soemthing, the "hook," to remember. Usually, the "hook" is also the name of the song, but not always.

How, exactly, you build your song will depend largely on how you are packaging yourself as an entertainer. If you start out sitting, you might be standing by the second verse. If you begin with small hand gestures, your gestures might become larger as you become more emotionally involved with the song. If you use dance in your performance, your steps ought to become larger, more intense at appropriate places in the song.

The bridge and the chorus of your performance should create a breakthrough which your performance emphasizes. If your song has two bridges, the second should be different, stronger than the first. Grow and, when appropriate, bring your audience down. Take your audience on an emotional journey

... entertain them!

Section 3D
Vocal Performance Tips

Take Care of Your Best Asset ... Your Voice!
Take care of your voice. Your voice should never hurt. Going on tour? Working in a nightclub? Are you required to perform 4-6 times per week? Regardless if your genre is musical theater or rock and roll, if your throat hurts from singing (and you're not sick with a cold or the flu): you are not singing correctly.

Suggestion: if you lose all or part of your voice or if your throat hurts do 2 things:

First, contact your doctor, preferably an ear, nose, and throat specialist.

Second, contact a reputable vocal coach — a vocal coach to teach you how to sing correctly utilizing your "mixed voice," during transitions to higher notes instead of straining or belting out those higher notes. As your "mixed voice" muscles develop, your range will increase, and you will gain more vocal control. With a developed "mixed voice," you should be able to seamlessly travel from low to high notes, and, at the same time, protect your best asset, your voice!

What is mixed voice?
Technically, there may be no such thing as "mixed voice." However, for purposes of this song performance text, I refer to "mixed voice" as imagining or feeling as if you are mixing the use of your chest voice and your head voice together at the same time.

Note: mixed voice is the opposite of singing from your throat ... missed voice is singing from your yawn. Proper use of mixed voice allows a seamless transition from low notes to high notes because the yawn opens instead of squeezes your vocal chords to produce the sound.

It is not uncommon for a singer to add a complete octave to his range by imagining using mixed voice, particularly toward the top of the singer's range.

Head voice doesn't have anything to do with any particular musical pitch. Rather, head voice is determined by the position and use of the vocal cords and larynx (voice box). Although the use of the term "head voice" varies widely among voice teachers, for purposes of this text, head voice is when your larynx is open and the width between your voice" varies widely among voice teachers, for purposes of this text, head voice is when your larynx is open and the width between your vocal cords allows sound to flow easily.

Don't know from where you are singing? One clue to determine if you are successfully singing in "head voice" is when you feel like the sound is vibrating in your head rather than in your chest. Thus, the term "head voice."

How do you learn to sing in mixed voice?
It's all in the yawn! Literally, practice singing and yawning at the same time. In order to "yawn," open your mouth wide with a deep inhalation (while taking in a deep breath). Begin to softly sing as you exhale a yawn. Don't sing loudly (leave it to the microphone to amplify). Find a teacher who knows and understands how to teach you to sing using your mixed voice.

For a more scientific approach, my friend and renowned singing teacher, Lisa Popeil, reminds me that yawning is the shaping of one's resonators (lifting the soft palate, lowering the larynx). And while it's true that laryngeal lowering makes it easier to sing with relaxed vocal folds – the act of yawning is primarily a way of creating a deeper (laryngeal lowering) and less nasal (the lifting of the soft palate) sound. Thanks Lisa!

When should you sing in mixed voice?
Unless your genre is opera (where only men usually use Falsetto or head voice), you should consider using "mixed voice" anytime a song takes you close to your natural upper vocal range (or what is sometimes called your "breaking point"). Even heavy metal performers find mixed voice helpful in their repertoire.

Why does it take so long to learn to sing in mixed voice?

It takes time to develop your mixed voice. Your muscles are not trained to sing in mixed voice. If you are just learning to sing in mixed voice, it should sound terrible. Don't give up. Slowly but surely you will build up the volume of your mixed voice. Practice, practice, practice until your muscles strengthen and you develop a mixed voice you can count on!

Note: Let the microphone and sound equipment provide the volume. If you are singing correctly, you will be able to convey all of the emotions of a song without high volume. It's your career ... don't spoil it by ruining your vocal cords.

Warm up: Baaaa
You are a singer or you want to be. Hopefully that means you enjoy singing. So, it should not feel like work to warm up your voice.

Driving to you next performance? Turn off the radio and sing to yourself and your companions. Sing in a soft voice focusing on the enjoyment of warming up your voice. One particular exercise that I often suggest for warming up a voice is the Baaaa exercise, below. You will find it not only warms up your voice, but it can help you develop beautiful additions to your vocal repertoire.

The Baaa Exercise: Although this is not a text on singing, per se, one way to develop your voice is to sing like a sheep. Yes, like a sheep! Baaa! Say it: "Baaaaaa!" Do you feel how your throat vibrates? Pick up a favorite song and try to sing softly your favorite part of the song using the baaa sound for every lyric.

The Baaa exercise is a beginning exercise that can be a first step to developing your tremolo, vibrato, and note tags. For the pro, i tis a great, safe, warm up exercise.

Ask your voice teacher or performance coach about this baaa exercise. Of course, I made up it's title, etc, but your teacher can help you further develope use of this most simple exercise. Or, just practice ithe Baaa exercise on your own. Almost everyone knows the children's song "Mary Had a Little Lamb," Use that song as your "baaa" exercise, singing every word of that song softly with the baaa sound.

Remember, seek professional help from someone who can prepare your voice with easy to learn vocal techniques that will not do permanent damage to your vocal cords.

Dynamic Song Performance

Mary Elizabeth McGlynn & John Michael Ferrari
Photo by Pepper Jay

One of the most talented singers I have ever had the pleasure to work with is Mary Elizabeth McGlynn. Mary is not only a voice artist for song and anime but she is an ADR (automated dialogue replacement) director. I remember recommending Mary to her first singing job on a video game (Top Gun: Fire at Will / Danger Zone). Mary so wowed the public and the entertainment industry that she now has scores of video game credits on her resume.

Vocal Microphone Techniques
Key: Don't pop your consonants into the microphone.
If your microphone is too close, the audience will hear the popping noises of your consonants. Consonants are the English letters: b, c, d, f, g, h (sometimes), j, k, l, m, m, p, q, r, s, t, v, w, x, y, and z. If too much breathe passes over the microphone the vibration is heard over the speaker system. Therefore, although it is crucial to always enunciate your consonants, don't let your consonants be distractions like little bombs going off in your microphone.

Key: No extra pre-pops here!
Prevent the pre-pop sound that occurs when you open your mouth before each lyrical phrase. Close your mouth shut. Now, open your mouth quickly. Hear the "pop" sound? That's the pre-pop sound picked up by the microphone (and the audience or recording equipment) before each lyric if you close your mouth and open it right before your first word.

Here are two suggestions on how to cure pre-pops: Either keep your mouth open (preferably smiling at and connecting with your audience members) or, if you do close your mouth between lyrical phrases, open your mouth again a second before the lyric (when, hopefully, the music will camouflage your pre-pop sounds, if any.

Always carry Chapstick© or some other thick lip balm, which helps prevent the sound of your lips opening.

Key: Don't hide your mouth with the mic.
The best microphone placement is when the top of your microphone is opposite the front of your chin. Not only will the audience be able to see your lips when you sing, this placement of the mic will prevent your consonants from exploding into the mic. If you are one of those singers who must "eat the mic," try to perform often at 45 degree angles to your audience so they can see your mouth once in a while.

Your audience wants to see your lips. Some audience members will read your lips as you sing. Others will simply enjoy the sensuality of watching your lips move. Your lips convey emotion. Covering your lips makes it harder for the audience to connect with your emotion and with you. Whatever the reason, when you cover your mouth with the microphone, you deprive your audience of one of your sexiest attributes ... your lips!

Stop The Pops Exercise: After you record yourself
practicing with your microphone, listen for any "popping" and re-record yourself until you are satisfied that the "popping" has disappeared.

Watch Your Lips Exercise: After you record yourself singing with your microphone, watch your lips. What are your lips communicating? Are your lips inviting? Smiling? Interesting? Experiment with different expressions. Create vulnerable lips by relaxing your jaw and allow your lips to naturally fall open and be soft. Create interesting lips by opening them ever so slightly so that you are showing the whites of your top two front teeth.

Practice, practice, practice. You are in the best position to learn what your lips and mouth are communicating to your audience.

Use Your Short Vowel Sounds
Short vowel sounds are usually more pleasing to an audience and they assist with better communication of the song's meaning.

Vowels are the following English letters: a, e, i, o, u, and sometimes h. Each of the first 5 vowels possesses both long vowel sounds and short vowel sounds. The long vowel sounds are usually symbolized with a short straight line (¯) above the vowel. Examples of the long sounds are: a - plane, e - key, i - nine, o - bone, and u - tuba. The short sounds are usually symbolized with a short convex curve (ᴅ) above the letter. Examples of the short vowel sounds are: a - apple, e - egg, i - insect, o -orange, and u - umbrella.

Some consonant combinations also provide the choice of long or short sounds. The short sound will almost always be more pleasing to the ear. An example is the song classic, "Crazy" written by Willie Nelson and made famous by Patsy Cline. The first lyric, "Crazy" may be pronounced two ways. The long sound of "zy" is "zee." This is actually how Patsy sang the song: "Cray-zee, I'm cray'zee for feeling so lonely." Listen to the difference if, instead, you use the short sound of "zay" or "zeh."

Sing, "Cray-zay, I'm cray'zay for feelin' so lonely." The use of the short "e" vowel sound softens the harshness of the long "e" vowel sound. Also note that, in the short vowel example, I also dropped the "g" from "feeling" to become "feelin'," which also softens the lyrical phrase and i s popular with many country singers in particular..

Successful country singers rarely sing the harsh "ing" portion of a lyric. Instead, they soften the lyric ending to "in," which gives the song more of a country feel.

Open Your Mouth
All great singers open their mouth to sing. You may think, "of course one has to open their mouth to sing!" But, actually, you would be surprised to observe that most unprofessional singers try to sing while opening their mouths as little as possible. All types of professional singers want to take full advantage of an open mouth during singing. An open mouth is not just for "belters" and opera singers.

Open Your Mouth Exercise: Although you will not usually want to sing in your speaking voice, it is good practice to over-open your mouth during practice singing: sing while opening your mouth just as wide as if you were speaking to someone far away and then open your mouth even wider as you continue singing.

Vocal Control

With "mixed voice" in your arsenal of vocal talents, you gain control of your voice. You are able to seamlessly sing from your low notes to high notes without a noticeable break in your voice.

You no longer have to pull the microphone a foot away from your mouth to prevent your high notes from blasting out. You no longer have to squeeze out your high notes with a tight throat and a constipated face.

With "mixed voice," gone are the days when you have to sing louder, or "belt" it out, so as to hit the high notes.

Please don't confuse this vocal control concept with microphone techniques used for effect! Sometimes it's fun to pretend a note is difficult to hit.

Note: When in a recording studio, real-time vocal performance skills save time, energy and money. Poor skills require many takes," and extra "star dust" to be added on to the recording by studio engineers during the post-production process.

Dynamic Song Performance

Adam Lambert & Allison Iraheta American Idol,
Season 8 (2009)
Photo courtesy of Associated Press

Note: "If you want to be a famous recording artist, your voice must be unique and immediately recognizable." Kara DioGuardi, American Idol Judge, Season 8, said this to the world about contestant Allison Iraheta, "You just hear one note and it's undeniably Allison!"

The Uniqueness of Adam Lambert, well, is Adam Lambert ... enough said! Allison toured twice with Adam Lambert (also of "American Idol,Season 8"). Subsequently, Allison and Matthew Hager formed a new band, "Halo Circus." "Halo Circus features Allison Iraheta as lead vocalist, David Immerman on guitar, Matthew Hager on bass, and Veronica Bellino on drums. Their first hit single was "Gone." In 2014, "Halo Circus" was covered by most of the entertainment industry trades including The Rolling Stone, Hollywood Reporter, and Variety. With their album, Bunny,". is gratifying to witness my students transforming their performance dreams into their reality. Adam has been an excellent friend to Allison since their meeting on "American Idol".

Section 3E
Body Movement - Complement the Phrasing

Keep it Interesting
Key: Share all sides of you with your audience.
A live or video taped singing performance is a visual medium. Keep your audience interested visually. Every so often, give your audience a different part of you to look at. When you sing to audience members sitting to the right, you share the left part of your face with the audience members on the left. To the contrary, if you always sing facing forward, the audience never gets the other views of you. Keep your performance interesting. Of course, multi-camera performances help capture all sides of your performance.

Blending of Physical and Vocal Communication Key: Perform with all of your body parts to complement the phrasing of the lyrics.

Use your body and hand movements to introduce a phrase. Give the audience something to look forward to. For example, if the lyric is, "I don't get no satisfaction ...," you, as the entertainer, might begin with a slight left-to-right shake of the head, as in "no" and then direct your fingers slightly toward your chest, just prior to singing the first words of the lyrics, "I don't get no satisfaction ..." This "blending" of the physical and vocal communication of the song adds depth and meaning to the lyrics and interest to the performance and increases the entertainment value of the song and the entertainer.

Blending, in effect, mimics "real life." In "real life," whatever that means, we usually do not know what we are going to say until we say it. Often, prior to speaking, our first reaction is a slight delay to internalize new information or gather our thoughts. During this delay our face involuntarily communicates what we are internalizing, accented by a slight, sometimes unconscious, physical gesture, such as a slight shrug of the shoulder, tip of the head or an almost grin. Once we've gathered our thoughts, we communicate verbally, or in song parlance, we sing the lyrical phrase.

Thus, "blending" more resembles "real life" resulting in a closer, more intimate relationship with your audience. Create thoughts between the lyrics. What do your lyrics mean? What are you sharing with the audience? Add to the mix the "blending" of slight physical gestures as you begin your lyrical phrase and your song will spring to life.

"Blending" is a key song performance skill. "Blending" is the ability to learn to communicate the song with all of you, not just your voice, but with all of you. It is a true sharing with your audience. Remember, what you think shows on your face.

Note: Avoid continued use of literal movements. For example, no need to hold up 3 fingers every time you sing "three." No need to point to the sky when you sing about the moon. Too many literal movements may be interpreted as boring, or worse, as condescending by the audience. Use literal movements sparingly and change them up with each pass of the chorus.

Congruence
Key: Keep your vocals and body in sync.
Objects that are exactly the same size and shape are said to be congruent or "in sync." Excellent entertainers perform with their song and their body "in sync." The performer's movement complements the words and music. In contrast, when your body is moving one way and the song or the music is going in another direction you are disconnecting from your song and from your audience. The two ways to stay congruent are to move with the music and be true to the lyrical phrase.

For example, if you are raising your arm during the last note of a song, keep that arm raised until that note is complete thereby keeping your arm movement and the note "in sync." Or, if you are moving across the stage during a lyrical phrase, time your movement so that you stop as the lyrical phrase is completed. Competent use of congruence provides a more polished performance.

Experience The Music.
Know your music. How does the music "feel" to you?

Is the music: strong (forte, **f**) or very strong (fortissimo, **ff**) or soft (piano,**p**) or very soft (pianissimo, **pp**)?

How fast or slow is your music? What is the music's beat, or time signature? The top number in a time signature tells the singer how many beats per measure there are in the song. For example, a 4/4 time signature states that there are 4 beats per measure. In ¾ time, there are only 3 beats per measure, etc.

Dynamic Song Performance

What is the "pulse" or the driving beat of the music? Find the beat that seems the strongest to you. Usually the rhythm section of the music or the bass line play the "pulse" beat of the song. The beat of the music is what makes you want to move. How does your music make you want to move? Does the music inspire you to want to dance? To clap? To march? To sway?

Allow your body to naturally move to the music. Whenever your song is devoid of lyrics, such as the introduction or instrumental, or the instrument phrases between lyrics, your body should continue to communicate the music to your audience.

An aside: I first begin working with Melinda del Toro when she was about 14 years old. This young Latina has now garnered many fans from all over the world as she managed to weave her loveliness into the hearts of people of all ages. If you have the opportunity to watch Melinda perform, notice how her body seems to naturally move to the music and with the meaning of the lyrics.

Melinda del Toro
Photo by John Michael Ferrari

Deaf Man's Introduction

Key: Allow a deaf person to "see" your song through your mood and body movement during the song's musical lead-in. The introduction to your song should do just that: introduce your song. That includes introducing the genre, tempo, and mood of your song to the audience. During your song's musical introduction, pretend the audience is deaf. Communicate the intro through your own thoughts, mood, and body movement. Allow your "deaf" audience to experience the beat and attitude of the song during its intro. In fact, an added gift to your "deaf" audience is to also communicate the dynamics and essence of your song during its musical phrases and instrumental portions.

I Just Can't Get My Body to Move To The Music Exercise: If you are one of those people who just doesn't move well with the music, start slowly with this exercise and be kind to yourself.

Stand with your eyes closed and listen to the music. Take your time and feel the music. Picture the music in your mind's eye. If the music is relaxing, relax. If the music is pounding, feel powerful. Begin to tap your foot to the "beat." Easy? Now, instead of your foot, move a different part of your body to the beat, and then another, then another, one body part at a time. Keep your eyes closed as you "dance" one body part at a time to the music.

This exercise can become quickly exaggerated and silly but it can be helpful for those of you who still experience a disconnection between your mind and body and between your body and your music.

Be True to the Lyrical Phrase

Each of your movements when performing should match or be congruent with your lyrical phrase. Your movement should be timed so that it is completed when your lyrical phrase comes to an end. Your movement that accompanies and accents that phrase should not end before or after your lyrical phrase ends. You've heard of hand-eye coordination. When you are true to your lyrics, you develop movement-lyric coordination.

Step-by-Step Example:

I will use three classical lyrical phrases to explain: (1) "Somewhere," (2) "over the rainbow," and (3) "way up high." Decide what body movement you want to utilize for each phrase. For example:

(1) "Somewhere," could be preceded with a slight shrug of the shoulder, shake of the head, and/or palm up in an "I don't know where" gesture that would last the lyrical phrase, "Somewhere." Or, your movement to "somewhere" could be as small as a subtle gaze on the horizon.

(2) Your hand could motion slightly over your head, from left to right, subtly drawing a rainbow while singing, "over the rainbow." Or, your movement could be small as a large knowing smile dignifying your success at imagining yourself reaching the other side of the rainbow.

(3) Separately, to emphasize the height of the rainbow (the height of the dreams the rainbow signifies), use a large arm movement palms up rising to the sky during your lyrics "way up high." If each of your ovements lasts as long as the phrase that the movement describes, your body movement and lyrics have achieved a conguency that is comfortable for your audience.

You are in effect, pantomiming the emotion behind the lyrics, providing your audience with a visual as well as an audio performance.

Dynamic Song Performance

John Michael Ferrari
Photo by Pepper Jay

An aside: I met John Michael Ferrari when he was performing at Highland Springs Resort near Palm Springs, California in 1990. What I noticed as I watched John sing and play guitar was the unabashed joy he had for performing. I had no idea that my son would invite John for dinner the next evening, which gave me the opportunity to make John a proposition. I would teach him performance skills and produce his original songs in exchange for a piece of the action. At dinner, I almost changed my mind when I saw John dip his bread into his wine. But I didn't, and as a result, you can enjoy John Michael Ferrari's songs on iTunes and John live onstage with the "oldies" band, "Ferrari & Friends."

End Freeze
Key: Wait for the payoff.
Always end the song with a strong meaningful movement, a motion that gives finality to the song performance. It can be a strong large hand and arm movement. Or, when appropriate, a small close of your eyes and bend of your head toward the ground movement.

Whatever your final move, hold your final position past the end of the song at least 3 - 5 seconds, if not longer. This "end freeze" provides a strong ending to any song. This "time out" allows yourself to feel the moment, to catch your breath if necessary, and begin to hear and enjoy the audience's appreciation for your performance. Your end movement should not last longer than the beginning of the dying down of the applause.

Acknowledge Your Audience
After the "end freeze," acknowledge and thank your audience. Each acknowledgement will be directed to different parts of your audience in a systematic format. If your audience includes a balcony or upper sections, your acknowledgments should include those audience sections. The actual words and movements you use will depend on your style. A rather simple straight forward example of acknowledging your audience might be:

1. Facing center, "Thank you," with a slight bow.
2. Facing right, "Thank you very much," slight bow.
3. Facing left, "Thank you," slight bow and wave. For larger audiences, add:
4. Pointing or waving to the upper sections, "Thank you up there."

The applause must last longer than the acknowledgments. In other words, you, the performer, should not get caught thanking an audience after the loudest portion of the applause begins to wane. On the other hand, audience acknowledgements may always start up again or continue after the applause has almost died down. This is particularly true if someone, such as a master of ceremonies ("MC") joins you on stage to thank you for your performance. If you have a reason to remain on stage, such as to introduce the next act or simply to chat or "patter" with your audience between songs, do not wait until the applause has ended before speaking.

Some of us relish the kudos and good feelings from our audience. Others feel self-conscious about receiving the accolades. If you feel awkward standing in front of an audience that is appreciating you, get used to it! It is, or should be, one of the best aspects of being an entertainer. Your audience is enjoying itself when, as a group, it is clapping, smiling, and appreciating you. The greatest feeling is when your audience is clapping and looking at each other in amazed appreciation. That was the goal of your audience when they gathered to become your audience in the first place; to be pleasantly entertained!

Section 3F
It's All in Your Eyes and Facial Expressions

Eye Contact
Key: Eye contact connects you to your audience. Wikipedia defines "eye contact," in part, as "an event when two people look at each other's eyes at the same time. It is a form of nonverbal communication and has a large influence on social behavior... "Eye contact is your direct connection to your audience.

An uninteresting singer almost certainly has "dead eyes" or "vague eyes." This may occur from an unfocused gaze, not really looking at any particular audience member or audience section but rather looking in a vague direction toward the audience. Or, the singer may, in "real life," avoid eye contact and continues that habit during performances. Whatever the reason or excuse for inadequate eye contact, the result is disastrous. An audience interprets "dead eyes" or "vague eyes" as disinterest in the song, disinterest in the audience, and lack of self-respect.

Chris Martin / Coldplay Courtesy of Associated Press

Chris Martin songwriter and front man for the band, Coldplay, sings with such sincerity that he transforms his audience into his imagination. Chris will sometimes effectively use "vague eyes" as a performance tool, but only for a moment.

Allow Your Face to Express the Lyrics
Key: Your face should give your song away.
Before you sing the lyrics, your facial expression should disclose to your audience what to expect. You know when something is right or wrong with a person even before they speak. You "see it on their face." Their thoughts and emotions are "written on their face." Their facial animation reveals the yet-to-be-sung lyrics.

You are what you think. The best and easiest way for your eyes to communicate your lyrics is to think about the meaning of the lyrics before you sing them. That split second of thought will express itself in your eyes and face.

When you learn to express the lyrics in your face before you sing them, your song will come as alive as if you were having a real conversation with your audience. If any one song performance technique separates the good from the greatest, it is the skill to communicate a song with all of you, especially your facial expressions. Be an actor and use the lyrics as your script!

Thought Exercise: Draw a line down the center of a page. Write or type your lyrics, double-spaced on the right side of a page, with a lyrical phrase for each line. On the left side of the page, in front of each lyrical phrase, write a brief thought. Memorize not only the lyrics but also your thoughts (or un-sung lyrics). Your thoughts are just as much a part of your performance as are your lyrics. You can change up your thoughts with different performances of a song and those changed thoughts will result in different performances.

Example of thoughts preceding lyrics using "Because of You" by Kelly Clarkson with David Hodges and Ben Moody.	
Pre-lyric emotional thought	**Lyric**
I am depressed	Because of you I will never stray too far from the sidewalk
I am angry at you	Because of you I learned to play on the safe side so I don't get hurt.
I am angry with myself	Because of you I find it hard to trust
I am lonely	Not only me, but everyone around me
I miss you	Because of you I am afraid

Fun Action Song Exercise: Choose a song that you think has fun descriptive lyrics. Record yourself "singing" the lyrics 3 times. First, sing the lyrics with over-exaggerated and animated thoughts and facial expressions. Don't forget to briefly think about each lyrical phrase before you sing it. Second, sing the lyrics ONLY with your facial expressions ... no singing. Third, sing the lyrics with animated facial expressions that

are not over-exaggerated; sing as though you were "on stage." Our favorite song choices for this exercise are classic TV theme songs from the 1950's or 1960's; such as "The Ballad of Gilligan's Isle," written by George Wyle and Sherwood Schwartz. Any song you choose that includes fun descriptive lyrics will work perfectly for this exercise.

Note: Shortcut thoughts into a few one-word categories. Apply those short thoughts, when appropriate, prior to singing lyrics. These one word thoughts could be as simple as happy, sad, lonely, afraid, excited, desirous, questioning, loving, angry, nervous, etc. Not only do the thought shortcuts take less time, but also some performers find them easier to use than trying to internalize the meaning of each lyrical phrase.

Chapter Four.
How to Move On Stage

Stay Balanced

Move Your Chi (aka: The Pendulum Method)

How to Walk On Stage

Introduce Yourself to Your Body

Choreography – Create an Act

"You have heard: 'He can't walk and chew gum at the same time!'
"Well, don't let that be you!" – Pepper Jay

Dynamic Song Performance

Section 4A
Stay Balanced

Key: Own your stage. You are an athlete.
Like an athlete, you, the singer, must also strive to always be physically balanced, with your weight evenly distributed between your two feet. This is true even during choreography where, for example, your legs are in a "lunge position" (one leg straight and one leg with knee bent as to lean; lunge). With few comedic and dramatic exceptions, an audience will feel uneasy when a performer appears to be leaning or unbalanced on stage. That stage is yours; own it!

Basic Dynamic Performance Foot Positions

Position One – Truck Driver Position

Position Two – Left Pivot

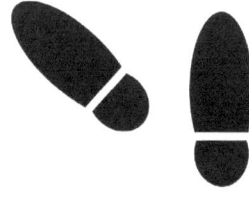

Position Three – Right Pivot

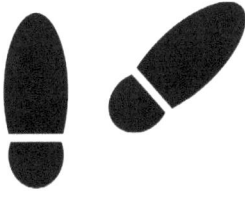

Balance Exercise

1. Begin standing in what I call Position One – the "Truck Driver Position," with your weight evenly distributed between your feet, which are spread no wider than your shoulders. Turn your toes slightly in. Your knees should be slightly bent or at least not locked shut. Now bounce slightly. Feel the bottom of your feet evenly balanced. Two parts of each foot should feel the floor: sole and heel.
2. Now, pivot (swivel) your left foot slightly to the left so that your left heel is pointing to the middle or instep of your right foot. (I call this Position Two or Left Pivot.) Now, bounce slightly. Are you evenly balanced? If you are not balanced, adjust your feet and/or weight until you feel completely balanced and comfortable. Keep your knees easy.
3. Return back to Position One.
4. Once you feel yourself completely balanced, pivot your right foot slightly to the right so that your right heel is pointing to the instep of your left foot. (Position Three or Right Pivot). Bounce slightly.
5. Continue this exercise with your feet going from Position One to Position Two to Position One to Position Three … over and over again until you feel balanced during every part of your performance.

Record Your Legs/Feet Exercise

Practice performing your song in front of a camera that is focused on your legs and feet. What positions do you use? Would an audience see you as a "balanced," in-control confident performer or a performer that is unbalanced and unsure? Watch for common mistakes such as putting most of your weight on one leg while the other is trying to balance on one toe.

Remain Secure

The audience picks up on your every move. If you are swaying from side to side, having nothing to do with your song or if you are nervously pacing on stage, you transfer your nervousness to your audience. Remain physically secure and solid. Stand and walk with the purpose of communicating your song and patter to your audience. Commit completely to your movements by making them precise (whether hard or soft movements) and by allowing the movement to mirror and complement the lyrical phrase.

Return to Center Front

Your beginning and end positions, unless required by your perspective of your song, should be center front or what is described as "downstage center" (see Parts of a Stage chart, below). The area of the stage away from your audience is called "upstage." You should avoid entertaining from the upstage area, unless required by the context of your song. When you are located "upstage," you are the farthest possible distance from your audience.

Note: Parts of a Stage: The names of the parts of the stage are from the point of view of the talent (actor/singer/dancer]. When standing on the stage looking out toward your audience, stage right is to your right. Stage left is to your left. Downstage is closest to the audience. Upstage is behind you toward the back wall of the stage.

```
                          UPSTAGE
   UP RIGHT                                         UP LEFT

                        CENTER STAGE
     RIGHT                                            LEFT

   DOWN RIGHT          DOWNSTAGE                    DOWN LEFT
                        (Audience)
```

Work the Stage Exercise
1. Unless your song begins during your entrance onto the stage, begin your performance downstage center. Sing to all sections of your audience, including the camera, before moving. How long you stay downstage center depends upon the tempo of your song and the size of your audience. If your audience includes balcony sections, it may take 7 or more phrases before you've shared a portion of your performance to everyone.
2. Move to downstage right center (about ½ the distance between downstage center and the far right end of the stage). Remember to keep your sternum (chest bone) pointed at least slightly toward your audience and to move with your microphone in the hand that allows your audience to see most of your face and sternum as you are moving. Physically travel on your stage either (1) between lyrics or (2) in musical time to a complete phrase(s) of the lyrics. Once you've arrived at your chosen downstage right center position, again sing to all sections of your audience, giving special attention to those nearest you, before resuming your journey across your stage.
3. Return to downstage center. Sing to all sections of your audience and your camera before moving again.
4. Move to your chosen downstage left center position and repeat Step 2, above.

Return to center front.
It is important to end your performance downstage center, unless the production of your song requires otherwise. End your song downstage center with a substantive grand finale and "end freeze."

Travel With or Between the Lyrics
There are two chief ways to move successfully on stage during a song:
(1) Move between lyrics and during the introduction to lyrics.
(2) Move in time to the lyrics.

If you are a singer/dancer, you already understand the concept of traveling on stage to the beat of the music. For the rest of us, it bears emphasizing the importance of retaining harmony between the performer and what is being performed. It is the congruence sought between performance skills and the music/lyrics. Practice moving to your music; the music you use to record your songs or when you perform live.
Note: The sophisticated singer is able to separate traveling on stage as well as the movement or action from the lyric itself. For example, if the lyrical phrase is "Here comes the cavalry," the movement or action before the lyric might be a look toward the distance with an out-stretched arm and finger pointing to where the cavalry is coming from, followed by your face and eyes returning to an audience member before sharing the lyrical phrase "Here comes the cavalry."

Exercise to Music Exercise: Exercise to the music you perform. This allows your body to involuntarily learn how to move to your music. All parts of your body. Do you stretch? Stretch to your music! Stretching to your music is the best because it allows you to move the individual parts of your body with your music. What would you look like swaying side-to-side to your music? What would alternate back shoulder rolls look like enjoying your music? Do you jog? Jog to your music. If you don't dance, but might like to learn, or even if you do know how to dance, practice dancing to your music ... all different kinds of dances, both

formal and silly. As performers, we all should be on some sort of doctor approved exercise program. Include moving to your music as part of your exercise program.

The Space Belongs to You
The stage upon which you will perform is yours. It is up to you to choose to be as large or as small as you want to be on stage depending upon how you wish to communicate your song. You can point to the ceiling with an outstretched arm. You can crouch and share a private moment with your audience. Be creative. Be comfortable with your movements. Movement includes using any space you can reach.

When I am about to perform or lecture on an unfamiliar stage, I think to myself, I wonder what my stage and all of its space will look like. My stage. My space. It all belongs to me. That thought, alone, gives me confidence in any new location. Study your stage, if possible, before your performance.

Section 4B
Move Your Chi
(aka: The Pendulum Method)

Key: Song performance movement is a 3-step process: mind, energy, and motion.

If performers appear awkward on stage, they are probably using only a 2-step process to move: mind and motion. Employing a 2-step process, they think, "I want to move my right arm upward." and it moves. Yes, the arm moves upward but it does not flow as well as it could; the motion does not fully communicate. Instead, the movement simply travels from one location to another. Sounds rather dull, does it not?

Compare moving your body in a 3-step process. Your mind moves your energy and your body simply involuntarily follows that energy. Your movement becomes a meaningful, powerful, and believable sharing of the song; your movement is "in sync."

For purposes of this text, we will call this energy of life your "chi." The vital force believed in Taoism and other Chinese thought to be inherent in all things.

The Chi Exercise:
Step One: Find or create your chi; the location in your body where your energy source sits. Sit comfortably, with proper but relaxed posture or lie down on something restful. Turn off the light, close your eyes, and block out everything around you. Relax and try to enjoy any sounds you may hear. Listen to your body. Without moving, try to identify where you carry your energy. What feels heavy (not necessarily fat, just heavy). Is your energy centered in your stomach area? Your chest? Your nose? Your head? If you can't find your chi ... No problem!

For purposes of song performance skills, you can "make up" where your chi is located. If you are a female and you can't locate your chi, imagine your energy source to be in the center of your stomach (think Madonna, Janet Jackson, or Ann Margaret; expressive and sensual).

If you are a male and can't find your chi, imagine your energy supply to come from the center of your chest (think John Wayne, Will Smith, or John Travolta; proud but elegant).

Once you track down or create your "chi," you are ready to move your chi.

Move Your Chi Exercise:

Step 1: Turn off the lights and/or close your eyes. Locate or "create" the location of your "chi."

Step 2: Relax and allow your mind to command your energy to transfer your "chi" to another body part. Stop. What is it like to feel your "chi" in another body part?

Step 3: Repeat Step 2. Experience the movement of your energy from one body part to another.

Step 4: Turn on the lights, turn on the music you perform to, stand in front of a mirror or a camera or both and Repeat Step 2. Allow your body to follow the energy as you enjoy your music. As you imagine your energy source traveling from one body part to another, how does your body change, how does each of your body parts with the energy respond to the music?

Note: For purposes of this exercise, do not voluntarily move your body. Just think about moving your energy. Use your thoughts and imagination. Allow your body to involuntarily follow the energy.

The Pendulum Exercise: Imagine that your "chi" is a pendulum inside of your stomach ... moving from side to side. Imagine it slowly swinging to the right of your body and then swinging to the left of your body. It might help if you think of the movement as a sideways "figure 8" movement. Allow your body to move with "figure 8" thoughts. Slowly, move the pendulum higher into your chest. Imagine the pendulum swaying in your chest to the right and then to the left. Allow your body to involuntarily follow. Move the pendulum higher, up into your neck and shoulders and allow it to slowly swing from right to left, right to left. Move the pendulum up to your head and move the energy of the pendulum slowly right and left. Repeat the exercise, slowly lowering the pendulum down the body until it swings in your thighs. By now, you should start to experience fluid movement; movement with purpose.

Note: If you consider yourself disconnected from movement, slowly do the Pendulum Exercise at least 2 minutes daily. This is a particular good exercise to record in order for you to view yourself. Do you see yourself a little bit differently than you imagined?

Movement derived from energy is movement without awkwardness. You will be amazed at the possibilities of your movements. Your range of movement and the variety and specificity of your movements will increase. How far you can grow in movement is as extensive as the possibilities of your ideas. Your ideas translate on stage in limitless ways. Think outside of the box. What box?

Make Your Movement Your Own:
For example, heavy metal singers might use their arms and fingers like lightning ... shooting energy out of their fingernails so effectively that the audience thinks it sees the lightning, hears the thunder, and experiences the force of the energy.

Gospel singers might use their arms and hands to shield themselves from sin in such a dynamic way that the audience emotionally feels their struggle. Perhaps hip hop singers might touch their face in such a way that every teenager dreams it was his or her hand touching that face.

Entertainers use their energy to move their bodies, thereby strengthening their communication with their audiences. What is it that you wish to communicate with your song performance?

Reminder Note: If you still have trouble understanding the "move your chi" concept: don't worry! Relating to one's energy source can be difficult for many of us. That's why, if you can't find your "chi" naturally, just make up the location of your energy source and start the exercises from that point. Remember, you are what you think.

Follow The Energy Exercise: Part One: You Are a Detective
Pretend you are a detective and you carry your "energy" in your nose. You are always looking for clues. Close your eyes and think about putting your energy into your nose. Smell. What do you smell? Allow your energy to follow the smell. Relax. Without trying to move, think about moving your energy from your nose to your right cheek and back to your nose again, now to your left cheek and back to your nose. Repeat: nose, right cheek, nose, left cheek. Repeat.

As you think about your energy source moving you should notice your head starting to slightly move naturally from side to side as your cheek pulls the energy from your thoughts. Your neck reluctantly but involuntarily will follow. As you continue the exercise, the result is a beautiful fluid motion of the head. It is this graceful and flowing motion that the performer seeks to perfect!

Part Two: You Are a Boxer
Move your "chi" to your chest. Concentrate as you feel the power of your "chi" fill your chest. Pretend you are a boxer. Fighters are full of bravado and usually carry their "chi" in their chest area. Feel your chest expand with energy as you imagine the energy center in your chest. Now move your energy from one side of your chest and then slowly to the other side of your chest. Both your neck and lower body should begin to gently follow your energy source from side to side.

Try this side to side movement without moving your hips. The result is stylish isolation of the movement of your chest area. Don't forget your rib cage. Make your movement begin at the bottom of your rib cage. This rib cage movement creates different angles and provides your audience with more of you to see and enjoy. Whether you perform with large gestures or with subtlety, it is this stylish fluid motion that professional singers seek to perfect.

Practice moving your chi from one body part to another. Remember, if you don't feel it, just make it up as if you did feel yourself controlling the movement of your energy within. The more you practice moving your energy source, the more natural you will look to your audience during song performances.

It may well be informative to watch other performers you admire and determine how they move and carry themselves. Where do they carry their chi? How do they express their energy source? How do they move their chi?

Section 4C
How to Walk On Stage

Key: Walk with grace, purpose, and confidence. Whether keeping beat to a rap song or gently strolling to the introduction of a country tune, when you travel from one mark to another on your stage, your movement should:
1. Put the audience at ease with your confidence, acquainting your audience with who you are as an artist or as the role or character you are portraying.
2. Communicate the music to a deaf audience; and
3. Reflect the purpose of your song or at least the introduction of your song.

Walk on Stage Exercise: Record yourself as you practice walking to your music, stepping to the beat. Vary your walk. Walk on your toes, on your heels, high step. Practice with slow, medium, and fast tempo songs. For example, if the song is slow, such as a ballad, also practice walking "double time;" two steps to a beat. If the song is fast, like disco, also practice walking "half time," one step to every two or 4 beats. This is an incredibly important exercise for both professionals and want-to-be professionals. Make time to practice walking to the music.

Walk With Grace:
Find your chi (your energy source) and walk with grace using the energy source to guide you.

A female usually looks best when her source of walking is from her pelvis. Allowing the pelvis to lead forces your body up straight which translates as confidence. Allowing your back leg to stay back just a slight moment longer lengthens your leg, giving you a sleek look. Your chest and shoulders naturally follow. The result is grace.

A male usually looks best when his source of walking is from his rib cage. Allowing the rib cage to lead forces your top and your bottom to follow easily. The result is strong but graceful movement. Practice walking in front of a mirror. If you bounce when you walk, it will distract your audience unless bouncing is part of your act.

Walk With Purpose:

Your persona as an entertainer plus the beat and the subject matter of the song determine the purpose of your walk. What is the song about? Is it spiritual that deserves a slow, heavy walk? Is it 50's bubble-gum song that warrants a light carefree walk? As a singer, you are an actor ... you are acting out the song for the audience.

A portion of your song performance is the purpose you give the song by your choice of walk and movement

Part of walking with purpose is determining when to walk on stage. Some genres, like hip-hop or rap, may lend themselves to lots of walking and movement to the lyrics. Other genres, like pop, new age or folk, may yield a stronger performance by walking only during the introduction and musical interludes so that you are delivering the lyrics primarily from a stationary position.

Walk With Confidence:

When a singer walks clumsily on stage or across a stage during the performance, the audience becomes nervous and anxious. The audience senses the performer's inexperience. Practice walking. Record yourself walking.

Here are some Walk With Confidence don'ts:

1. Please do not slouch unless you are doing so deliberately for effect as a part of your act.

2. Please do not clump or stomp or shuffle unless you are doing so deliberately for effect as a part of your act.

3. Please do not perform in any shoes, whether high heels, boots, or whatever, unless you are accustomed to performing in those shoes.

4. Please do not perform in new shoes before you scrape or roughen the bottoms to prevent slipping, sliding and/or falling.

Begin Movement With Upstage Foot

When moving from one position of the stage to another, begin your movement with your upstage foot; your foot furthest away from your audience. Upstage refers not only to the rear of the stage but also to that portion of the stage away from the camera(s), if any.

For example, when traveling toward stage right, you would begin your movement with your right foot. The same is true when traveling toward stage left, you would first step with your left foot, instead of crossing over with your right foot.

At first, using your upstage foot to begin movement may seem unimportant to you. Nevertheless, try it and you'll quickly discover its importance. Stand facing your pretend audience and then begin your movement to the right or left with your downstage foot, taking one crossover step and STOP before taking the second step. What does your audience see? They see the back of your shoulder. By using your downstage foot first, your first movement literally closed off your body to the audience.

Exception: From time to time, a performer will turn away from the audience for special effect.

Section 4D
Introduce Yourself to Your Body

Key: Isolation of movement.
Isolation of movement is focusing your movement on principally one body part at a time. Isolation of movement is an advanced performance skill that separates the good from the excellent. In order for you to utilize your body parts in a performance, the first step is to remember that you have them to use.

If you have not already, please introduce yourself to your body. Introduce yourself to all of your part "assets;" those parts of your body that you could have in your arsenal of song performance tools. For example, your head, eye, smile, arm, hand, fingers, shoulder, hip, knee, etc. Once you remember you have these assets to work with, practice sharing them, one at a time, with your audience.

A subtle shoulder roll while looking at an audience member or section can be a powerful connection between you and your audience.

Isolation of Movement Exercise: As you perform your song for your "real" or "pretend" audience, use different body parts to send your "chi" to audience members. At first, begin by concentrating on only one body part throughout an entire lyrical phrase. For example, as you sing the lyrics, you also think to yourself, "You, to the right of my audience, take this set of lyrics from my right cheek (From my right cheek "chi".) You, in upper balcony center, grab this next lyrical phrase from the energy from the left side of my jaw. Hello, you in the left of my audience, you take my "chi" from my left ribs.

Give more of yourself to your audience. Give your audience energy from your body parts using isolation of motion. Whether with a subtle movement of a welcoming finger to a larger extended arm, allow your energy to guide the movements that accent your lyrics and music while, at the same time, being true to your branding of yourself as a performer.

Learn To Dance
Invest the time necessary to learn the basic dance steps of the beat of the music that you sing. Those who devote energy to learn the basic steps of their genre find the movement portion of their song performance skills improve dramatically. Learn to dance outside your musical genre and learn rap dancing, cha cha, fox trot, rumba, hip hop, dance pop, swing, and/or Gangnam Style.

For those with more advanced appetite, learn more advanced dance moves and incorporate all or parts of those dance moves, whether large or subtle, into your performance. Draw performance ideas from many styles and forms of dance. Create your own movement you feel and look "insync" and comfortable with.

Madonna
Photo courtesy of Associated Press

An aside: Madonna has to be one of the most creative singers, performers, and producers ever to exist. Not only does Madonna provide a different and unique entertainment experience with each album and performance tour, she has set a high standard of creativity for generations to come.

Advanced Dance Walk Exercises:

BOOGIE WALK: Walk so that each step begins with moving your free leg by lifting the hip and stepping forward.

SCUFF: Brush, sweep or scuff the foot against the floor (but do not leave marks on the floor!)

SLIDE: Take a step on one foot in any direction then draw or slide the other foot up to the weighted foot. James Brown is an example of this type of movement.

Repeat the above and enjoy finding your creativity.

Videos on the internet are easy ways to experience samples of every type of dance step and to listen to every type of beat. Use the Net to your best learning advantage.

Of course, some may say you do not really need to learn how to "dance" in order to perform well, as long as you can learn how to "move." I say, even if you're not interested in dancing, basic dance steps may help you become more acquainted with your body and may better ease you into basic types of movement you may not have considered for yourself previously.

Section 4E
Choreography: Create an Act

How to Share the Stage
Key: Create a fluid dance between players so each moment creates a photograph.

When two or more perform together, whether they are singers, musicians, and/or dancers, it can either add a positive dimension to a show or create chaos. A performer who knows how to share a stage, both physically and psychologically, will lift the entertainment to new levels of energy and excitement.

The Duo: The perfect singing duo is the interaction of two people taking turns as lead singer. Singing partners should watch and listen to each other as well as sense each other to be able to share the spotlight and alternate control of the stage.

When two singers perform together without knowledge of basic performance skills, it can often be uncomfortable for the audience. In the perfect combination, each singer incorporates all of the performance skills in this text. In addition, here are specific skills that allow a duo seamlessly share the stage:

1. Blend your voices. Match your partner's tonality, volume, and attitude. If one person has a soft tone to their voice, such as when singing in mixed voice, and the other person sings with a hard edge, such as when singing in straight head voice, the voices will not usually blend well. Singing partners must listen to each other and find a compromise between their voices that improves the performance c

2. Establish your relationship. The interaction between stage partners is of utmost importance. The duo's stage relationship should be clear to the audience. If the duo is comprised of two guys or two gals, the audience needs to understand they are best friends, siblings, or even rivals, etc., performing on stage together. A male female duo can create a relationship of brother and sister, flirtatious teases, friends, or romance, etc. Whatever the relationship, the audience will feel more comfortable when they are "in" on what the relationship is.

3. Direct the audience's attention. Body language and eye focus direct the audience to the focal point of the performance.

   When a musician has a solo instrumental, all others on stage should be enjoying, and, if possible, facing the soloist or, at least, partially turning toward the soloist. When possible, have your sternum (breast bone) and eye focus directed to the focal point.

   When your partner is singing, you can step back slightly and your partner can do the same when you take the lead. However, when singing together, be careful not to stand too far back on the stage, which may cause the other performers to turn their backs on the audience and thus get "upstaged." When the focal point of a performance is "upstaged," it not only hinders the interaction between partners but it also makes the audience feel uncomfortable. Confused audience members never know where they should be directing their attention resulting in a performance to end badly.

   Of course, rules are destined to be broken. An effective entrance may be made from unconventional locations: upstage center high upstage staircase, from the audience, itself, or even on a rigging dropping from the ceiling.

4. Patter between players. The patter between two people must usually be quick and must always flow easily with comfortable timing. Each person must listen to the other and pick up on punch lines or clues from the other and be able to respond accordingly.

   As in "improv," patter should follow the standard improv rule: "YES AND ..." Whatever your partner says, approve of it and

   add to it instead of negating your partner and going on to another subject. Unless you are performing a negative comedy routine, never undermine your partner's performance by making unflattering remarks to or about them. Be encouraging and complimentary.

   If your male / female routine includes "jabs," the woman should make the jabs, but usually never the other way around. Sexist? Yes, but true. The audience will usually take the side of the female. Even if you are doing a Burns & Gracie (George Burns and Gracie Allen) or a Lucy & Desi (Lucille Ball and Desi Arnaz) type of routine and the female is a little ditzy, or slow, make sure you show her respect and understanding even through your impatience. Your audience will be more accepting. Develop a relationship of complete mutual support.

5. Respect Your Fellow Performers. Whether you are on or off the stage, evidence your respect for other performers; whether dancers, co-singers, band members, or background singers. This is particularly true when the other performers are children or older people. Try not to "talk down" to them or to patronize them. My basic rule of thumb is to interact with young or elderly singers as you would any other professional performers. Try not to let their age get in your way. In other words, treat everyone with professional respect.

Photograph Your Performance
During your dress rehearsal and, if possible, during your performance in front of an audience, have someone take photos of you. Also, ask them to take photos of the other performers on stage with you and your partner if you are a duo. Take photos of you and your band or orchestra. Take photos of the entire stage. Lots of photos.

If someone continually takes photos with a digital camera, each minute of your song could result in hundreds of digital photographs. Or, better yet, have two people take photos of you and your fellow performers. One camera could be in the center of the audience and the other at the side.

These images of yourself performing will give you an opportunity to see what your audience sees ... one still photo frame at a time.

Ask yourself, do each of your performance "moments" create a beautiful or interesting photograph? Does each communicate to your audience what you intend to share? What are your strongest moments? What are your weakest moments? It is times like these when you should be critically honest with yourself.

Chapter Five.
Package Yourself

Mimic your Models Choose Your Style

Package Yourself as a Song Performer

Create a Fan Base

Demo Reels

Pay your Dues

Practice the Audition Process

Learn How to be a Photograph

"Branding is not just for cereal." – Pepper Jay

Section 5A
Mimic Your Models

Key: Find what you like in others and borrow, borrow, borrow.

So, you are or want to be a professional singer? Recording artist? Performer? Entertainer? Voice over artist? Choose your goal and be as specific as possible. Choose a group of people who are doing or have successfully done almost exactly what you want to do.

What do you admire about their performance attributes? Why? Be precise. Whom in your industry do you choose to be your inspiration(s)? Put together a mosaic of singing artists and their song performance skills that you would like to have for yourself. What would it take to practice copying some of those qualities you appreciate? Learn to mimic what you appreciate. Practice copying from each of them attributes you admire. You might take hand movements from one performer, a dance step from another, and a particular glance from yet another. Once you have internalized their song performance skills, adapt them to your own style. This method is also referred to as "modeling."

When choosing mentors to mimic or model yourself after, don't select quickly. Spend the time to watch numerous performances. Today, with YouTube, Vimeo, Ustream, Livestream, etc., and the public broadcasting stations, one could watch singers from several generations 24/7 easily and conveniently on your computer or phone.

Caveat: Do not limit your modeling choices to artists only in your musical genre of choice. The methods used to become a great entertainer are, more or less, the same regardless of whether your musical preference is rock, pop, folk, country, new age or rap. If you are weak on communication with the audience skills, find artists who communicate well with their audience and copy what they do. Most importantly, once you can successfully mimic your attribute of choice, adapt that skill to the type of songs you interpret and to your own personality; your own professional brand.

Dynamic Song Performance

Usher – photo courtesy of Associated Press

An aside: Usher is an American recording artist, dancer, and actor considered by many around the world to be one of the reigning Kings of R&B. Yes, Usher is a sex symbol but it is his unique vocal skills and communication with his audience that fill the arenas and creates the platinum records.

Over the decades, there have been many singers and performers, but relatively few great entertainers. My favorite entertainer of all time is Sammy Davis Jr. who sang, danced, and joked his way into my heart when I was only 6 years old!

Dynamic Song Performance

Here are a few samples of entertainers who have excelled in many of the Dynamic Performance Skills:

___audience connection of Britney Spears

___believability of Jennifer Lopez

___choreography of Fergie & Sammy Davis Jr.

___communication skills of Wayne Newton

___confidence of Justin Timberlake & Kanye West

___dance moves of Usher & Michael Jackson

___ease of Kris Kristofferson & Kenny Chesney

___facial expressions of Cee Lo Green

___focus and determination of Madonna

___grooming of Rihanna

___like-ability of Stevie Wonder

___magnetic stage presence of Miley Cyrus

___microphone techniques of Allison Iraheta

___originality of Lady Gaga & Steven Tyler

___perseverance of Gregg Allman & Michael Bolton

___phrasing skills of Sinatra

___production skills of Celine Dion

___sensual energy of Fergie

___sensuality of Toni Braxton

___sexy image of Christina Aguilera

___patter of Taylor Swift

___style development of Snoop Dogg

___song interpretation skills of Barry Manilow

___unpredictability of Norah Jones

___ voice production of Jose Jose

___vocal range of Diana Ross

Find what you like best in other singers and: Borrow, Borrow, Borrow!

Dynamic Song Performance

Barry Manilow
Photo courtesy of the Associated Press

Barry Manilow has always been a quadruple threat. Barry uses his songwriting, arranging, singing, and producing skills to create songs that last several lifetimes. Whether it's "Mandy" or "Copacabana," Barry's song interpretation skills continues to designate him the entertainer's entertainer.

Section 5B

Choose Your Style

Key: Ask critical questions about yourself.
Who do you want to be as a performer? What is your "style?" Choose a style for yourself. Become that style; become "it."

If you have not already, begin your questioning with, "What genre of music do I like"? Sample genres are rhythm & blues, country, jazz, pop, rap, hip hop, reggae, show tunes, lounge/rat pack, folk, world music, new age, or classical/opera. Each of these musical genres has certain traits. What are the characteristics of the music you want to perform? Most singers think they have addressed these questions but most have not dug deep enough yet.

Take a self-inventory: What are your talents? Do you sing on pitch? Does your voice remain strong as you sing at the top of your vocal range? What is your natural range of motion; what movement is your body already capable of doing?

Be honest with yourself about what you look like. What kind of music would a stranger think best describes your looks? What type of performance would your style attract? What type of style would your audience, your public, accept as true about you? What type of audience do you want to attract? Who do you want to be your fans?

Ask More Questions. What do you visualize about the performer you want to be? How do you sound? Are you the smooth-motion singer or the easy, swing-bounce singer? Are you a harsh or raspy singer? If yes, perhaps your musical genre is heavy metal or hard rock and roll or raspy blues; then your "style" would be harsh. When performing, you might utilize a low center of gravity that creates a base for rapid locomotion and quick direction changes, and sudden stop-actions that throw your body into bold, angulated shapes.

Ask these questions about yourself and choose your style from your answers to these questions. Once you have an inventory list of your looks, talents, and desires, choose your "style" or, better yet, adapt a "style" to be your own ... branding!

Dynamic Song Performance

Still can't decide what your style should be? Record yourself experimenting with different singing styles. (Put a wig on and have fun.) If you still can't choose which style is best for you, seek the advice of an experienced song performance coach or manager.

Fergie / Black Eyed Peas
Photo courtesy of Associated Press

An aside: Remember the lyrics of "Big Spender?" "Do you wanna have fun...fun...fun? How's about a few laughs laughs laughs? Let me show you a ... good time!" Well, that is what Fergie does on a consistent basis. Fergie combines her talents as a singer, delight and entertain her audience with her own brand of style.

Dynamic Song Performance

Develop Your Own Signature Style

Key: How do you want your fans to visualize you? Who are you, the performer? Here are some tips on how to find or develop your "own style." Please keep in mind that you want to create a style for yourself that looks like it "goes with you." You want to be memorable but, at the same time, seem natural and real. (Mick Jagger, the rock group, "Kiss," or American Idol's Adam Lambert are examples of the outlandish but believable). Also, choose a style for yourself that is long lasting; a style that you and your fans can live with hopefully forever.

Develop a signature style of your own.

Sir Mick Jagger – Photo courtesy of Associated Press

Dynamic Song Performance

Steps to creating your own style; your branding:

1. Objectively take a serious assessment of your overall current style when you sing. Do you prepare yourself or throw on whatever outfit may be semi-clean or easy? Decide what parts, if any, of your current performing style you want to keep.
2. Pick a general genre or a crossover genre for your style of music. Answers to these questions may be of assistance:
   - Where should the public look for you to purchase your music on iTunes, CD Baby, Sound Cloud, CD Universe, Spotify, Amazon, etc.? Country? Rap? Jazz? Alternative?
   - Do you want to appear traditional or preppy (such as a navy blue blazer, button-down Oxford-cloth shirt, cuffed khakis, and loafers)?
   - Do you see yourself as modern or fashion-forward? (Madonna, Pink, or Allison Iraheta would fall in this category.)
   - Perhaps you see yourself as a more casual GQ type (Barry Manilow or Notorious).
   - Or, do you want to be the hippie natural singer? (Janis Joplin, Jimi Hendrix, and Bob Dylan come to mind).
   - Maybe you want to sing narrative songs about your personal experiences (Taylor Swift or Johnny Cash).

Janis Joplin – photo courtesy of Associated Press

Dynamic Song Performance

The genre of music you choose will help dictate your style of clothes. Heavy metal singers, rappers or funkers lean toward t-shirts and hooded sweatshirts, paired with baggy 'skater' jeans and chains, Eminem comes to mind.

Eminem – photo courtesy of Associated Press

Dynamic Song Performance

Please do not forget about props. Britney Spears' belly button is a prop!

Britney Spears – photo courtesy of Associated Press

3. Take a closer look at your favorite singers. Which of their attributes immediately come to mind? Do they have a special sound? A unique look? A particular genre? What is it about them <u>you</u> want for yourself? You don't want to be a fashion clone. Yet, at the same time, do not hesitate to build off someone else's look and transform it into your own. Make sure that the look fits into your intended "singing performance" personality. No matter how conservative or crazy your look, you will want audiences to accept you and to like you and

Dynamic Song Performance

to remember you. The biggest success in this regard is to develop your own trend; develop a look that is uniquely your own.

4. Realistically decide what you would be most comfortable changing about yourself. Your hair color? Wardrobe? Accessories? If you are going to a different hair color or drastic hairstyle change, try out the look first in a wig shop. It is cheaper and less permanent than a haircut! Or, use a wig like

Susie Stillwell
Photo by John Michael Ferrari

5. Think about colors when you are forming your signature style. What colors look best on you? There are people who specialize in matching your skin tone, hair, etc. to certain colors. Before spending lots of money on a new wardrobe, it may be helpful to seek the advice of a "color specialist" or a "stylist."

6. When deciding on your signature style, design a style that covers up your flaws and draws attention to your best features. What are your flaws? Hips a little too big? Ears stick out? What are your best features? Beautiful hair? Great legs?

Jimi Hendrix – Photo courtesy of Associated Press

Dynamic Song Performance

7. Your signature style must complement your performance and your attitude must complement your signature style.

8. Think about one signature element you can adopt that is memorable. Some examples are Kayne's glasses, Lady Gaga's hair, and Britney's schoolgirl outfit.

Justin Timberlake
– photo courtesy of Associated Press

Style Tips for All Performers:

1. Shoes: Wear comfortable shoes. Performance shoes, even tap shoes, should be "slip on" or with straps. Stay away from shoes that tie. Stay away from rubber soled shoes that may stick to the floor and may be difficult to move in. Be careful when performing in new shoes with leather or other soles that can slip. New leather shoes should be well scuffed on cement or other rough surface or with sand paper prior to your performance.

2. Make your outfit efficient: Can you easily perform your entire routine in the clothes you have chosen to perform in? Watch out for loose material, as in large shirt sleeves or pant legs, which may accidentally get caught up in your movement or microphone cords, etc.

3. Does your signature style include a hat? Better make sure it's one that will stay on your head when it's supposed to. Practice your routines in the outfit you intend to perform in.

4. Show only what you want: When choosing your performance signature style, take into consideration the effect of the lights on your outfit. In some venues, the lights are so strong that many materials become transparent. Whether or not "see-through" is an aspect of your style, it is best to know ahead of time how the audience will see you.

Kiss – photo courtesy of Associated Press

5. Customize: If you go all the way to famous, even your silhouette will give away who you are. Michael Jackson used his silhouette to great effect. Once you've chosen your signature style, consider customizing your clothes or buying vintage. If your style is "signature" enough, just your outfit, or your makeup (Kiss) will give away who you are to your audience and fans.

Dynamic Song Performance

Michael Jackson
– Photo courtesy of Associated Press

This author is of the opinion that Michael Jackson, Sammy Davis Jr., Madonna, and Al Jolson were some of the best American performers of all time.

Good Management Helps Create Image
One of the most essential assets a professional singer must have in this industry is good representation. While a great responsibility lies on you, the performer, a good manager can be invaluable. An attentive manger will help you select your singing style and guide you through additional career image questions. How can clothes, hairstyle, and your body movements help translate your looks, desires, and talents into the style of performer you want to be?

Which subtle body movements are in harmony with the image you have chosen? How do you want your professional image to stand, walk, sit, travel up or down stairs, get into and out of vehicles? How should you speak, watch, and listen in public?

How do you determine your "style?

Begin by brainstorming. Write down all words you believe describe yourself as well as words that describe how you would like your style to be. Try not to limit yourself to sane or logical choices. Think conservative, wild, egotistical, even crazy. When brainstorming, there are no wrong choices. Ask others, trusted friends and family and your manager, if you have one, what words they might use to describe you and your singing.

From your brainstorming list, choose what you believe to be the 3 best words that might describe your performance "style" or "image." Choose words that describe how you would like to portray your singing career to the world. Once you decide which 3 words you will use, that is how the public will refer to you.

Your "style" is your professional branding. Make it easy for the public to remember you. With assistance from your management, select which of these sample "style" words would describe the singer you want to be and add to the list your own "style" words:

Agile	Angry	Charming	Clumsy
Composed/Cool	Creative	Cute	Edgy
Egotistical	Flexible	Friendly	Fun
Energetic	Entertaining	Extravagant	Extreme
Handsome	Happy	Healthy	Honest
Hypothesizing	Kind	Kool	Jolly
Meditative	Motivated	Mushy	Outrageous
Positive	Powerful	Precious	Pretty
Romantic	Sad	Sexy	Smooth
Soulful	Strange	Talented	Tender
Thoughtful	Vital	Wholesome	Zany

Still uncertain about your "style?" Discuss these 3 questions with your management or trusted friends and family:

When you are famous, how would you choose to be "branded?"

What is that one word or phrase that historians will include in your biography?

What few words pop into your head when you visualize your favorite singer?

Dynamic Song Performance

Here are some sample brandings for a few earlier amazing performers:

James Brown	The Hardest Working Man in Show Business
Johnny Cash	The Man in Black
Paul David Hewson	Bono
Elvis	The King
Gloria Estefan	The Queen of Latin Pop
Madonna	Material Girl
Michael Jackson	The King of Pop
Frank Sinatra	Olde Blue Eyes
Bruce Springsteen	The Boss

Bruce Springsteen
Photo courtesy of Associated Press

Section 5C
Package Yourself as a Song Performer

Who Are You: The Product?
You, the song performer, may not be the "real" you. As a performer, you are a product, a commodity offered for sale, someone that others are willing to invest in. I suggest you package yourself as "the entertainer."

Don't confuse your "on stage persona" with the "real you." Often, a singer who explodes with energy on a stage or in a recording can be quiet and humble when not "on stage." Singers known for sensuality in their performance many times are shy in real life.

When prospective audience members or prospective purchasers of your songs conjure up who you are ... what is the product they are describing? What do you look like, sound like? What emotion do you want your fans to feel when they hear or see you? What is your:

Attitude

Posture

Clothing

Make-up

Movement

Phrasing

Color Combination

Energy Level

Cher – Photo courtesy of Associated Press

Make Your Singing Performance Important Key: Make an entrance after being introduced.

If possible before you sing, don't let your audience see you prior to your entrance. Try to have someone introduce you. Your separate entrance after being introduced lends importance to your performance.

If you have to set up your equipment in front of your audience, your entire band could leave the stage and then re-enter the stage when your performance is to begin. Or, your band could stay on stage and, after a moment (or an instrumental), one of your band members could introduce you, "Ladies and gentlemen, [insert your name here]," followed immediately by the music.

You wait a beat or two and enter the stage using your song performance skills to greet your audience. Lights can also assist in lending importance to your performance. Lights could dim prior to your introduction or lights could change or additional lights could be added. These touches contribute an aura of mystery.

Frank Sinatra – Photo courtesy of Associated Press

Emotional Appeal
Your song takes your audience on an emotional journey. However, just the thought of you should invoke pre-planned emotional appeal. What emotions do you want your fans to feel when they hear your name? Excitement? Pleasure? Sensuality? Love? Importance? Friendship? How do you want your audience to be emotionally moved as they remember you? She's hot! He's funny! She's politically important! He's sexy!

If your dream is to be a superstar, I suggest your goal is to make your audience want to either be with you or to be you!

Get Help!! A Trusted Manager Goes a Long Way
One of the main jobs of a "Manager" is to package the singer. You, the singer, may not be the best person to make decisions about your career. This is particularly true when it comes to your own packaging. Putting yourself together as a product is like putting together a puzzle with the help of your trusted management. It is impossible to see ourselves as others do.

Dynamic Song Performance

When you find a manager or producer that you trust, follow their advice. Musical history is replete with examples of fortunes made when the singer was not allowed to make their own choices but rather forced to follow the judgment of others.

My favorite example is Sammy Davis Jr. who was often billed as the "greatest living entertainer in the world". According to his autobiography, "Yes I Can! The Sammy Davis Story," Sammy actually loathed both "Mr. Bojangles" and "Candy Man" and fought not to record either of those songs. "Candy Man," of course, became Sammy's signature song in his later years and Sammy's performances of "Mr. Bojangles" have always been one of my favorites!

A more current example is Allison Iraheta. Long before Allison was a top 4 finalist on "American Idol, Season 8" and a world-renowned rock star, Allison was a singing contestant on Telemundo's reality show, "Quinceañera." Quinceañera, in Latin American culture, refers to a girl's 15th birthday when the girl "becomes a lady."As the final episode of the singing reality show Quinceañera" approached, Allison was carefully following the performance directions of the show's producers and, although she was advancing in the rounds, she was not considered one of the top 2 finalists for the win. We advised Allison to do something the show's producers would have frowned upon.

The plan was to follow the producer's instructions during the show's rehearsal but when the 7 "live" cameras were rolling, to deviate from the rehearsal and perform just as she had been taught in my studio. We explained to Allison that the cameras would find her wherever she went on the stage, and it was more important to create a performance impact rather than please the producers and camera operators. I held my breath as I watched the TV and Allison began her final song of the contest, the wonderfully dynamic "Total Eclipse Of The Heart," by the talented Bonnie Tyler.

The song began and Allison stayed on her "mark" and the show's cameras followed her as planned. And then it happened. Allison pulled out all of the song performance skills she had learned. Immediately, the audience went crazy, screaming with excitement. Each time Allison moved around the large stage to better connect with her audience, the close up camera lost her, the video engineer went to a wide shot, and then another close up camera found her. That control room must have been in an uproar, but again and again during the song Allison amazed the entire audience until they were on their feet, a first for any contestant during the entire season of the show. The result? Allison Iraheta, at 15 years old, was the winner of Telemundo's"Quinceañera" contest viewed by millions of people. I still get teary-eyed with pride every time I watch Allison's final "Quinceañera" performance on YouTube!

Manager vs. Agent:
A manager "manages" as a career consultant. An agent gets the artist work. Technically, a manager is not supposed to sell the artist or the songs. For a percentage, usually 10-20%, management will help the artist make all of the major decisions for an artist's career: How the artist looks, what the artist sings, what contracts the artist should sign, what type of venues the artist will perform in, and when press releases are appropriate. The manager will form a strategy to guide the artist toward that artist's goals. A manager should assist in choosing professionals the artist should work with; voice coaches, make-up artists, clothes designers, performance coaches, etc.

As of the writing of this text, an agent in the United States, on the other hand, is limited to 10% of the artist's income. Your agent communicates directly with your manager. Your agent, usually with the assistance of an entertainment law attorney, handles all of the artist's contracts and bookings.

People often ask me how they should locate a great manager or agent. My answer is always the same. Find someone who is doing successfully what you want to do and find out which manager and/or agent they use. Many will not take you as a client without a track record. Be persistent. Keep knocking on doors of successful people. Don't settle for your Cousin Suzie.

Caveat: If your manager or agent does not produce satisfactory results for you within three (3) months, find a new manager or agent or both.

Double Caveat: Do not sign a contact with a manager or agent or anyone without having an attorney look at it first on your behalf. And, don't use an attorney recommended by the manager or agent you are contracting with.

Triple Caveat: Make sure the contract includes an easy "out" clause for you to change managers or agents if you're not happy with them.

Dynamic Song Performance

Allison Iraheta and Pepper Jay
Photo by John Michael Ferrari

Allison Iraheta at her own Quinceañera

Section 5D
Create a Fan Base

If possible, try to collect as much infomation as possible from those who enjoy your singing. Names, phone numbers, addresses, emails, social media, etc. Collect business cards. Freely share with your audience your website and all of your social media, Facebook, Twitter, YouTube, yes, even MySpace, all of your "official fan pages," your iTunes, Sound Cloud, ReverbNation, etc. Send out newsletters. Write press releases.

At the start of your singing career, begin the creation of your fan base. Usually a manager helps create methods for gathering fans but, if not, you, the singer, should take the time to create your own fan club. This can be as easy as having a sign-up sheet or asking that business cards be placed in a bowl or information cards to be filled out by interested audience members. Back in the day, I preferred a perforated card with a photo and information on the top (for your fan to keep) and the fan's information on the bottom of the tear off (for you or your management to keep), like the one I created for John Michael Ferrari, below.

John Michael Ferrari
Thanks you for joining him for an evening of fun and entertainment
Please complete the form below, and become a member of the
FERRARI FANS MAILING LIST
PJP *For additional information, including private parties, please contact:*
"Pepper J. Productions"
323-957-1168 Fax: 323-957-9215 E-mail: PEPJAY@aol.com

Please print clearly!   Please fill out this form and return bottom portion to the stage. Thank You!

Your Name:_____

Address: _____

City/State/Zip:_____

Telephone : (day) _____(nite)_____

Immediately, after each performance, post photos of you on stage, and of you and your fans, or just your fans.

ASAP after you receive a card or digital information from a fan, send something; a note, a flyer, email, or text, to each person who signs up to your fan club thanking them for joining.

Either inform your fan club members of your next gig or inform them that you will keep them posted when your next gig is scheduled.

Sending regular emails or flyers to your fan club will allow you to keep up with any changes of addresses that may occur and will help your "fans" not to forget who you were or where they appreciated you. But, don't send so many communications that you clog up people's inboxes. Always allow them to "unsubscribe." A nice extra touch is to send each fan an autographed photo or a discount code for your latest tune!

Internet
We now live in a Cyber-space world. Marketing opportunities seem to change every month. Try to purchase a domain: Your Name dot com. Or, if your name isn't available, a website of your own is always a good idea. Are you out there in Internet land? Take advantage of the ever-evolving online social and professional networks. ReverbNation, MySpace, Facebook, LinkedIn, Plaxo, CD Baby, etc. and include your own Twitter and RRS feeds. Can one successfully find you on You Tube, blip.tv, vimeo, dailymotion.com, digg.com; the list grows constantly. Create your own channel on each. And, don't forget about the big guy, Google and its ever-expanding applications.

Explore the interest for free press release sites. Also, take advantage of Scoop It and Newsle and other sites that allow you to post information about your career. The modern way of marketing oneself changes almost daily. There are a number of books available which will include the latest tips on self-marketing in this new digital age.

Section 5E
Demo Reel

Key: Keep your demo reel current and short.
At any time, be able to show your performance highlights via a current 1–2 minute demo on your phone, via YouTube, by linking to mp3 files, or by sending out CDs/DVDs.

If you sing in different genres depending on the "gig," have a demo for each; i.e., short engaging clips of 4 – 5 country songs on one demo and 4 – 5 rock n roll songs on another. Prospective employers do not always have an imagination. They need to see exactly what they think they want to hire.

Try to obtain a demo tape of yourself with fairly good production quality. It can be difficult for a prospective employer to appreciate your talent through bad sound or scratchy or blurred video. If possible, try to get a direct audio feed from a sound mixing board directly into your camera for quality audio.

Keep your demo reel with you or easily available. You should have your demo on your phone, on your own website, posted on YouTube or Blip.TV or some other easily accessible internet medium. There may also be internet sites that specialize in promoting your type of performance.

Note: Sometimes it can be effective to hand out mini-CD demos as business cards. Make sure your business cards have your website on them. Please make sure the information on your business card is easy to read (tan text on a black card doesn't work). And, make sure the text on your business card is large enough for older employers to read.

Record Yourself Always and Often
Key: Try to view yourself objectively; as a product. Record yourself in action, both out in the world and during rehearsals. Take the time to watch yourself on tape. Convince yourself: You are not watching yourself, the person ... you are watching you, the performer. Be critical ... be very critical.

Record yourself rehearsing as often as possible as if you were in front of a live audience. Include patter ... planned or idle chatter with the audience or specific audience members. Rehearse.

Remember, the key to successful song performance is believability. You know what believable looks like, sounds like, and feels like. The goal of recorded rehearsals is to believably make the song and the performance yours.

Ask yourself as you watch yourself on the tape of you performing:
- What do I see?
- Do I see myself as someone who is happy to be singing?
- Do I, as the audience member, feel that I, the performer, am communicating the meaning of the song?
- If it wasn't me I was looking at, would I find myself interesting to watch?

Improvise. Improvisation is to make things up and perform them without previous preparation; to react "on the spot." As a performer, be able to go beyond your song list and memorized patter. Learn to improvise ... so that you can evolve your show as it grows.

For example, what if someone drops a dish with a loud bang during your show? If you've practice improv, you should be able to quickly comment on the "crash" and go back to your show without missing a beat. If the crash occurs during your song, keep singing, but improvise a fun gesture sharing the crash experience with the audience. If you are very advanced, you can change the lyrics for that moment to accompany the crash comment.

There are numerous "improv" classes in every major city. The most famous are Second City and The Groundlings (I took classes at The Groundlings and loved every minute of it!). In addition to more independent improv classes, check the community colleges and night schools for classes. Of course, you can watch improv comedy online, but I suggest visiting improv comedy clubs to see up close and personal how the pros do it. I O Comedy in Chicago comes to mind.

Rehearsal tip: Turn the camera on anytime you are rehearsing. The best scenario possible is to have a video camera set up at all times, aimed with a medium shot at the portion of your space where you practice your performance skills. (Medium shot records you from the top of your head to your waist.) Record as many of your rehearsals as possible.

Caveat: Don't wait until you are on stage to "give it your all." Practice your best performances during your rehearsals.

Create A Safe Place to Experiment

Create a special haven to practice your craft. Your own space that hopefully is ideal for creative conditions. Your practice space must be a safe place; a place where you can freely video record yourself, make noise and refine your techniques. Your practice space could be in your room, the basement, garage, barn, or at your local school or park.

It's always a good idea to consider the happiness of your family, friends, and neighbors as you rehearse. If your space is too close to others, try to rehearse through headphones or in a soundproof room. Rehearse with a microphone as often as possible. Many cities have affordable soundproof rehearsal rooms to rent inexpensively.

In your space, create your pretend audience and practice with them. You can imagine your audience or you can create a faux audience. Some ideas include drawing a mural of an audience for the walls, placing photos of audience members around the room or, if the walls are off limits, using stuffed animals as audience members. I often use stuffed animals as audience members during coaching sessions!

Practice talking to your audience and pretend they talk back to you.

Dynamic Song Performance

Danika Quinn
Photo by John Michael Ferrari

Section 5F
Pay Your Dues

At some point, it is time to practice your song performance skills in front of a live audience. Karaoke clubs are perfect places for both the beginning singer and the professional singer to practice incognito. (Wigs are great for this.) Check the karaoke club directory in your area. Or, if you are really a beginner and want to learn without your Uncle Harry walking in, sometimes it's better to take a friend and practice in karaoke clubs outside of your area!

Put together free back yard shows with your friends, senior citizen centers or retirement homes. When you've practiced enough, invite more of your friends and family. If you are young, get your parents involved. Get all ages involved and make a production out of it! Children love to help out and can make great audience members.

Practice often and wherever. Find safe venues to learn your craft. Years ago, a singer could choose from a multitude of local venues to practice their singing ... to try out their skills on live audiences, whether or not they got paid for the gig.

Nowadays, often a singer does not have many choices of local venues to experiment in. Think out of the box. The key is to create venues for yourself. Depending on your style or image, consider the following places to sing, whether or not they presently have singing entertainment: schools, churches, parks, restaurants, bars, coffee houses, hotels, malls, farmers markets, street fairs ... the list is as long as your imagination. And, remember, collect "fans" wherever you go so that you can call or email them the next time you perform.

When starting out, sing for free or for "tips." Enjoy the process and give yourself a chance to develop as an entertainer and to refine your song performance techniques.

Wherever you perform, ask the venue if you can bring in a camera to record your performance. If yes, bring a friend with you to record while you're singing. As you later review your taped performance, you should find that you are your best and worst critic. Try to be honest with yourself ... very few others will be!

Dynamic Song Performance

AL BOYD
Photo by John Michael Ferrari

Soul Singer and Composer Alphonso Boyd is always asking me, "what did you think of my performance? Anything I should improve upon? Meanwhile, Al has 9 Gold and Platinum records to his credits with such artists as The Temptations, Elton John, the O'Jays, Fish Bone, Etta James, Phoebe Snow, and Areosmith, to name a few. He has performed with several groups including The Imperial Wonders and Ferrari & Friends. A true professional never tires of truthful feedback!

Section 5G
Practice the Audition Process

Key: Fear is your friend.
Is auditioning out of your comfort zone? For many, the opportunity of an audition is accompanied by fear. Not to worry. That audition fear can be your friend. Your fear is telling you that you are experiencing, growing, improving, and exploring new things. Fear creates adrenaline. Channel that energy into your audition performance. As you learn and improve upon your song performance skills, your confidence level improves and your auditioning fear decreases. Scared? Learn to love it! Like learning to walk, just take one small step after another, learning one performance skill at a time. The result is confidence.

A special note on fear: If you're really scared ... and you know who you are ... smile and breathe. That's right, put on a huge smile and take a very large breath. That smile and breath should force your body to involuntarily slow down your heart rate, calm the acid feeling in your stomach, and lessen your desire to flee. Smile and take a big breath slowly exhaling. Repeat until you feel calm and you feel your heart slow. Remember that singing professionally is what you want to do.

Utilize all of your song performance skills in the audition, particularly your audience psychology skills. Perform for those at the audition just as if you were performing at whatever venue or for whatever recording you are being auditioned. Don't hold back in the communication of the song.

Caveat: "Blow Them Away," but don't blow your audience out of the room. Unless you're into a genre a la heavy metal, in any venue your loudest audio should go only to the walls and not bounce off of them.

Specific audition hints:

1. Your audition begins when you leave your house. Feel ready. Be appreciative. Be happy. Bring a special sparkle to your eyes and smile on your face. Be accommodating to others sharing your road, path, or elevator on the way to your audition. (The guy in the elevator that you didn't say "good morning" to could very well be the casting director or venue manager.

2. Be nice to everyone at the audition site. Make eye contact and smile to others waiting to be auditioned. Give respect and credence to the assistants running the audition. Truly appreciate the audition opportunity.

Caveat: It is not uncommon for the casting director, producer or assistant to sit in the lobby to observe the talent waiting to be auditioned!

3. When called, walk into the audition space as if you're walking on stage. Feel friendly and enter with confidence, visually acknowledging those in the room with a smile in your eyes. Those auditioning you want you to "be the one."

4. When you enter your audition location, greet those present. i.e., "Hello." Or, "good morning." Or, "Hi, I'm__." Then, add a quick tag giving your interviewers an extra few words about you and your speaking ability and speaking voice. I.e., "thanks for seeing me." Practice this.

5. Inside your audition, listen then respond. When asked to state (or slate) your name, spell your first or last name if it is unusual. After you state your name, add a very short tag that's comfortable to you and one appropriate to the situation. This short tag, a few quick 3 or 4 easy to understand words, gives those auditioning you an extra moment of your personality. And a quick smile and interaction before the "real audition" begins.

    I.e., "My name is__, thank you." Or, "I'm__, thanks for having me."

6. Use ALL of your song performance skills in the audition, making them appropriate to the audition space and camera.

7. Make sure your music is not louder than your voice. Don't make it difficult for them to hear you.

8. Thank them at the end of your audition. If there are several people in the room, try to give a quick nod or eye contact with as many as you comfortably can.

9. Don't rush your exit. Exit as you entered, with confidence, good posture, and at a regular pace. Try to make eye contact and smile at anyone you pass on your way out.

10. Have an audition notebook with you. After each audition, but before you leave the site, note the date, location, & purpose of the audition and the casting director or venue manager. Also, if you know them, note any names of anyone else in the audition room.

11. When you arrive at your car or when you get home, write down what you did well and what you didn't do so well. Be specific. I.e., "I entered well. I think they liked me. But, I rushed my lines again. And, I don't think I listened as well as I should have. I will do better next time."

12. And, most importantly, if you did poorly, don't dwell on it. Learn from it then move on.

Specific interview or red carpet hints:

Many of the audition hints, above, will serve you well when you are being interviewed, whether in depth or briefly on a red carpet. Here are a few of my special interview / red carpet suggestions:

1. Always begin with a compliment. Say something nice to the person interviewing you. Whether you enjoyed something they did, or remark how beautiful their suit, dress, or jewelry might be. They don't expect this brief compliment and, as a result, will probably provide you with a better interview.

2. Prepare ahead of time the points you intend to share in your interview. If you are on the red carpet, prepare a different brief "story" or "experience" to share with each reporter or media crew. This will keep you interesting, as a talent or celebrity, and the reporters will remember and be more interested in interviewing you in the future.

3. You determine what you share on the red carpet. If you have a publicist, they should assist you in writing a few bullet points to cover as you speak to media crews along the carpet.

4. Know your interviewer. If you know ahead of time who will be interviewing you, try to find out something about them. They like that!

5. Be humble and share credit. Bragging never looks good and looses its charm quickly. A response to any compliment should come in two parts. First, thank you. Second, giving credit to whoever helped you in order for you to receive the compliment in the first place. You may be thanking the cast or crew or director of a movie, the band or your music producer, the choreographer of your music video, etc. Thank one or two of them in each of your interviews. Prior to your interview prepare who you are going to thank and for what.

Note: In a sit down or exclusive interview, prepare a list of all of the people to think as well as the 3 short stories or pieces of information you intend to share.

Lady Gaga - Photo courtesy of Associated Press

Be Confident:
Remember my mentioning earlier to name your chair and to own the floor? Lady GaGa is a wonderful example of an artist who owns her space. You should enter every audition, interview, or performance location, believing that the area you are entering belongs to you. You own the floor under your feet. The walls are yours. And, if you have to sit at any time, that chair belongs to you.

One of the first things I ask a new student to do is to name their chair. As I mentioned earlier, the name of my chair is "Harvey." Any place I go, I wonder what my Harvey is going to look like. Sometimes Harvey is wood and hard. Other times, my Harvey may be soft and comfortable. Whatever Harvey looks like, he belongs to me. He is my chair. Knowing that I own the chair, I can sit back in the chair comfortably with my back feeling the back of Harvey if he has one. If Harvey has arms, I can feel them and enjoy the arms because they belong to me. The result is the appearance of confidence.

Knowing that the audition room, recording studio or concert hall belongs to you and that the chair in that room or hall is yours, will not only increase confidence, but will give the impression that you are confident. Own your space and name your chair.

Caveat: Be very careful when naming your chair because this should be the name of your chair throughout your entire career. Welcome your chair as if you've arrived at a safe place. I love my Harvey.

When I think of confidence, I am reminded of a story my Grandma Lida told me as a child. It was about a young doctor. He had recently graduated from medical school and finished his internship. The problem was he was scared to death about the idea of seeing patients by himself. Until then, there had always been someone

What advice did my Grandma give him? Pretend. You know what a doctor looks like. You know what a doctor sounds like. You know the confidence a patient is supposed to feel with their doctor. And, you have all the knowledge needed to be a doctor. So, pretend. Yes, just pretend and dress, sound and express like you think a doctor should be. Then, before long, you won't be pretending any longer. Soon, without you even realizing it, you've become the doctor you've always wanted to be.

Is confidence difficult for you? Pretend! Yes, pretend you have confidence. Owning your chair and the floor and the room is a good start!

Section 5H
Learn How to Be a Photograph

Key: Angles and Airholes.

If your goal is to be famous, you will want to know how to be photographed both on and off the stage. The key is to place your body in such a way as to create angles and airholes. Angles can be as simple as a slight tilt of your head or as dramatic as a side lunge. Airholes are those spaces that are created by the position of your arms and legs. You might want to refer to them as "air spaces." For example, when you place your hand on your hip, you have created an airhole between your body and your arm. You have also created an angle. When your feet are apart, you have created a space of air between your legs and the ground.

Beyonce – Photo courtesy of Associated Press

Paris Hilton and Beyonce are excellent examples of stars that know how to photograph well. Paris takes the time to physically pose for each photographer (and wherever Paris and Beyonce go ... photographers follow). Beyonce creates a spectacular photograph during almost every moment of her performance.

With each pose or movement, create body positions using angles and air spaces thereby providing each photographer and the audience with a shot that they, the photographer, and their fans, and you, can be happy with.

Angles and Airholes Exercise: Look through fashion magazines, particularly the advertisements, and you will discover that almost every model poses in such a way to create angles and air spaces! Notice how the models create angles with a tilt of their head or with some other part of their body, arms and/or legs. Notice how the models create airholes (space) between their legs, with their arms, or with their bodies and objects, such as a wall or tree or another person. Also notice how models often use their rib cages to create interest. Your body can fashion a slight angle by slightly moving your rib cage to one side and keeping the lower part of your body stationary.

On or off the stage, your attitude is captured in photos. Photos should communicate your "image" and "style." Your photograph should convey what you want your audience to remember about you. Are you a "stud" or "sex kitten?" Are you the squeaky-clean girl next door or the healthy athletic type? Is your music smooth or raw? Your mind-set will help direct your audience and fans to the image of you that you and your management seek from your public.

Off The Stage: You are walking out of the grocery store or on the red carpet and a fan with a camera or paparazzi calls your name. You should have practiced ahead of time how to turn to the camera so that the photograph taken will be the kind of photograph you want it to be.

How not to be photographed: When the photographer calls out to you, you turn your head to the camera, smile, and "click" the photo of you is taken. What is wrong with the photo? The turn of your head, without a turn also of your body, creates ugly lines on your neck and, even if you have a turtleneck on that covers the lines, the photograph will still look like your head is growing out of your shoulder.

How to be photographed: The best way to naturally "pose" for the photographer is to follow the same song performance rules you use on stage. After your head automatically looks to the camera and smiles, turn your body so that your sternum is facing the camera. Take a step so there is at least a slight air space between your legs and do something with at least one of your arms, such as a wave or grab of one of your lapels, both of which create angles and airholes. Turn your nose a little to one side or the other of the camera. Add a tilt of your hip or a slight lean and you have created an interesting photograph. Practice with someone taking pictures of you. It's easier to do this with digital cameras than it used to be with film. Remember: angles and airholes!

How to Be a Photograph Exercise. Record yourself with a series of still photographs.
- Stand with your shoulder to the camera looking straight ahead.
- Pretend that someone has called your name.
  Quickly look toward the sound and move into position following the steps in "How to be a photograph," in the preceding paragraph.
- If you sing as a duo or trio, practice taking photographs together as you create interesting angles and airholes using all of your body parts! Practice exaggeration.

- **Note:** If you have a good body, don't let a photograph hide that fact from the camera. Unless going for an artsy look, take photographs with your arms at least slightly away from your body so that your audience will appreciate your "figure." A photograph taken with your arms at your side usually makes you look "wide" or at least, wider than you actually are. Also, a photograph taken with your
arms down by your side often looks boring ... like a vacation shot taken by your Aunt Millie.

Experiment to discover what makes you look the best you can and goes best with the professional image you are trying to create.

Is your body not perfect? Your legs will look slimmer and more interesting when they are not so close together that they are touching when you're being photographed.

When being photographed and you are asked to look directly into the camera, a photograph usually looks better if your nose is pointed just to the edge of the camera lens. This makes a difference of only about 1/8 of an inch but, with your eyes directed to the center of the camera lens.

That 1/8'" will usually provide the camera with a better view of your nose

- Point your nose to the right or left edge of the lens.

The image above, represents the camera lens. Look into the center of the camera lens. Then, while looking directly into the center of the lens, experiment with your nose to the left edge of the lens ... to the right edge of the lens. Have someone take photos of both ways, with your nose slightly to the right and with your nose slightly to the left, and then determine which is your "best side!"

Mimic the Best: Watch celebrities walk down the red carpet. Most have practiced how to walk, how to wave, how to smile so that, at any given moment, they may be successfully photographed. Notice that they turn their body slightly toward each camera, one camera at a time.

On The Stage:
Key: Every moment is a photograph. Plan your performance so that, at any moment, an audience member can take a great photograph of you.

From the second successful entertainers enter the stage until their final exit, they would take an execellent photograph at each and every moment of their performance.

Someone who is famous is always "on," with high energy and keen awareness of their body positions and how they look to their audience.

Frame-by Frame Exercise: Record yourself performing a song. During playback, stop the tape or video frame by frame. If each frame were a photo, how would you look in that photo? That is the way you look to your audience during your performance. Video feedback can be the best feedback for the critical eye!

Repeat the How to Be a Photograph Exercise, above, during a practice performance of each of your songs. Just ask a friend to click away with a digital still camera. Ask them to take as many photos of you as possible. Each moment of your performance could and should be a photograph you can be proud of. I emphasize this skill again here in the text because this may be the best exercise to specifically dissect, analyze, and improve upon each moment of your performance.

Conclusion

Music has a special place in our lives. From the beauty of leaves rustling in the trees, to the sounds of a city street, to a 100+ piece orchestra elevating sounds to the heavens, music is everywhere. If you have the special gift of song, use your talent to enhance the beauty within you and the beauty of life around you.

Break a leg! *

*A well-known saying in theatre which means "good luck. Typically said to actors before a stage performance. It reflects a theatrical superstition in which wishing a person "good luck" is considered bad luck. It is thought that its' origin comes from the time of Shakespeare's plays when actors would receive tips on top of their salaries. Coin "tips" were tossed on stage by the audience during the final bows or curtain call, depending on how well they enjoyed the performance. In some bad performances, they would throw rotten vegetables. Actors would bow in such a way to 'take a knee', effectively breaking their leg line, on stage first to receive the applause and second to pick up the money. 'Break a leg' refers to wishing the actor success in their performance so in the end they would have to kneel down and collect a welcoming tip.

Appendix 1. - Dynamic Song Performance Helpful Hints

Believability is the key to performance.

Give individual audience members non-verbal attention and you gift your entire audience. Communicate the lyrics as if you mean what you are singing.

Carefully choose when to close your eyes during a performance. Do it sparingly.

Keep your vocals and body in sync. End the song with a strong movement.

Walk with grace, purpose, and confidence. Your face should give away your song.

Sing to and for your audience, not to yourself.

Don't eat the mic. Allow your audience to see your lips!

Mimic what you admire in your models. Like an athlete ... stay balanced. Develop your own signature style.

Wear comfortable performable non-tie shoes. Record yourself always and often.

Perform with your sternum (chest bone) to the audience.

Begin movement with your upstage foot.

Keep voice comfortable and relaxed when singing.

Find the performer within you.

Choose a voice teacher or performance coach with a track record in whom you have confidence.

Appendix 2. – Photographs

Talent	Photo Credit	Page
Thurston Watts, Allison Iraheta & John Michael Ferrari	Pepper Jay	vi
Allison Iraheta, Matt Hager, Pepper Jay	Jeff Knight	viii
Sophie Tucker	Maurice Seymour N.Y.	3
Pepper Jay	John Michael Ferrari	5
Billy Joel	Associated Press	8
Gwen Stefani / No Doubt	Associated Press	10
Allison Iraheta	John Michael Ferrari	11
Allison Iraheta & Halo Circus		12
Bono / U2	Associated Press	14
Garth Brooks	Associated Press	16
Prince	Associated Press	17
Laura Martin Cover Album Photo	John Michael Ferrari	18
Pepper Jay & Danika Quinn	John Michael Ferrari	22
Thurston Watts (Rest in Peace)	Pepper Jay	26
Golda Berkman & Pepper Jay	John Michael Ferrari	27
Kenyatta Mackey	John Michael Ferrari	30
Danika Quinn	John Wright	35
Luisa LuBell	John Wright	37
Celine Dion	Associated Press	44
Allison Iraheta & John Michael Ferrari	Pepper Jay	49
Brandon James	John Michael Ferrari	51
Al Boyd	John Wright	52
Mary Elizabeth McGlynn & John Michael Ferrari	Pepper Jay	57
Adam Lambert & Allison Iraheta American Idol, Season 8 (2009)	Associated Press	61
Melinda del Toro	John Michael Ferrari	64
John Michael Ferrari	Pepper Jay	67
Chris Martin/Cold Play	Associated Press	69
Madonna	Associated Press	85
Usher	Associated Press	92
Barry Manilow	Associated Press	94
Fergie / Black Eyed Peas	Associated Press	96
Mick Jagger	Associated Press	97
Janis Joplin	Associated Press	98
Eminem	Associated Press	99

Britney Spears	Associated Press	100
Susie Stillwell	John Michael Ferrari	101
Jimi Hendrix	Associated Press	102
Justin Timberlake	Associated Press	103
Kiss	Associated Press	104
Michael Jackson	Associated Press	105
Bruce Springsteen	Associated Press	108
Cher	Associated Press	110
Frank Sinatra	Associated Press	111
Allison Iraheta & Pepper Jay	John Michael Ferrari	114
Allison Iraheta	John Michael Ferrari	114
John Michael Ferrari	Ellis Photography	115
Danika Quinn	John Michael Ferrari	120
Al Boyd	John Michael Ferrari	122
Lady Gaga	Associated Press	126
Beyonce	Associated Press	128
Russell Watts, Thurston Watts & John Michael Ferrari	Pepper Jay	139
Pepper Jay	John Michael Ferrari	148
RJ	John Michael Ferrari	154

Appendix 3. – Sample Show Format

50 Minute Cabaret Headliner Show

1. Opening: fast & light; medium tempo
2. Bouncy, throw away
3. Sweet, quiet ballad
4. Big Moment
5. Novelty; not too heavy; slow-medium
6. Ballad type
7. Upbeat; fun
8. Strong Point; personal statement; original
9. Up Beat
10. Up Beat
11. Big Ballad / Show Tune
12. Encore

Appendix 4 - Exercises

Dynamic Song Performance Exercises	Page
Think, Internalize, Share, the Make it Look Real Exercise	31
Speak The Words Exercise	32
Speak The Words Differently Exercise	32
Strong Enunciation Exercise	33
How Do I Take In Information Exercise	42
Study Yourself Exercise	44
Three Step Punch Exercise	45
Phrasing Exercise	48
Make Love Not War with the Music Exercise	48
Over-Exaggeration Exercise	51
The Baaa Exercise	56
Stop the Pops Exercise	58
Watch Your Lips Exercise	58
Open Your Mouth Exercise	60
I Just Can't Get My Body to Move to the Music Exercise	65
Thought Exercise	70
Fun Action Song Exercise	71
Balance Exercise	74
Record your Legs/Feet Exercise	74
Work the Stage Exercise	75
Exercise to Music Exercise	76
The Chi Exercise	77
The Pendulum Exercise	78
Follow the Energy Exercise	79
Walk on Stage Exercise	81
Isolation of Movement	84
Advanced Dance Walk Exercise	86
Angles & Airholes Exercise	129
How to Be a Photograph Exercise	130
Frame by Frame Exercise	131

working on my book

Dynamic Song Performance

Ferrari & Friends
Russell Watts, Thurston Watts, John Michael Ferrari
Photo by Pepper Jay

Glossary

Terms As Used In
Dynamic Performance Skills

"A cappella"	Singing without instrumental accompaniment.
"Accent"	An emphasis or stress given to a syllable, lyric, or note. The relative prominence of a musical note (especially with regard to stress or pitch).
"Airhole" or "Air Space"	That space created by your body or your body and an object. I.e., if you put one of your hands behind your head, you have created an airhole (or space) between your arm and the side of your head. Or, when your feet are apart, you are creating an "airhole" between your legs and the ground.
"Audience Psychology"	The performer's study of the perceived mental processes and behavior of the performer's audience. The understanding of what techniques the singer may utilize to positively improve your audience's reaction to the singer.
"Auditory"	Of or relating to the process of hearing.
"Believability"	The quality of being credible or trustworthy. Achieved when an audience feels the singer's lyrics are authentic to the singer.
"Blending"	The complementary use of vocal and physical and emotional performance skills to add depth and meaning to the lyrics.
"Break a Leg"	A well-known saying in theatre which means "good luck. Typically said to actors before a stage performance. It reflects a theatrical superstition in which wishing a person "good luck" is considered bad luck. It is thought that its origin comes from the time of Shakespeare when actors would receive tips on top of their salaries. These coin "tips" were thrown on stage by the audience during the final bows or curtain call, depending on how well they enjoyed the performance. In some bad performances, they would throw rotten vegetables. Actors would bow in such a way to 'take a knee', effectively breaking their

	leg line, on stage first to receive the applause and second to pick up the money. 'Break a leg' refers to wishing the actor success in their performance so in the end they would have to kneel down and collect a welcoming tip. From Wikipedia, the free encyclopedia
"Charisma"	A personal attractiveness that enables you to influence others [syn: personal appeal, personal magnetism]
"Choreography"	Artistic planned dancing or movement; the representation of the song through planned movement.
"Chi"	Energy of life. The vital force believed in Taoism and other Chinese thought to be inherent in all things. The unimpeded circulation of chi and a balance of its negative and positive forms in the body are held to be essential to good health in traditional Chinese medicine. -ORIGIN Chinese (Mandarin), 'air, spirit, energy of life'. Also ch'i or Qi or qi
"Congruence"	Agreement and harmony between the performer's words, body, and emotions; when it all "goes together" well. Mathematically: coinciding exactly when superimposed one upon the other.
"Consonants"	Any letter that is not a vowel. For purposes of this text, consonants are the following letters: b, c, d, f, g, j, k, l, , w, x, y, z. While it is always important to enunciate all consonants during a song, you should always be aware of not "popping" your c's, k's, p's and t's into your microphone.
"Cover Band"	A band who sings and/or records songs first recorded or made popular by someone else.
"Dynamic"	Marked by action, intensity and vigor; forceful or force of personality; an efficient incentive.
"End Freeze"	Those 3 - 5 seconds at the end of the song where you hold the final moment before breaking into thanking your audience.
"Enunciation"	Mode of pronunciation; articulation; to speak and sing clearly so as to be understood.

"Falsetto"	A singing technique that produces sounds that are pitched higher than the singer's normal range. Technically, "falsetto" is produced when the vocal folds of your vocal cords vibrate in a length shorter than usual, where part of your vocal cords does not make contact with each other.
"Ferrari-ism"	A word or phrase, real or made up, used by John Michael Ferrari and/or Pepper Jay when coaching Dynamic Song Performance Skills.
"Foot Positions"	For purposes of Dynamic Song Performance, refer to these foot positions: Position One – the "Truck Driver Position," with your weight evenly distributed between your feet, which are spread no wider than your shoulders. Turn your toes slightly in. Your knees should be slightly bent or at least not locked shut.
"Genre"	A type or class; A category of artistic composition, as in music or literature, marked by a distinctive style, form, or content -French, from Old French, kind, from Latin genus, gener.
"Head Voice"	Head voice is not associated with any particular musical pitch, but rather with the position and use of the vocal cords and larynx. Technically, when singing using your "head voice," your vocal cords are thin and have wide amplitude. Head voice allows singers to increase their range and is partially achieved by lowering the air pressure below the vocal chords to prevent going into falsetto. Many singers feel that when they sing in their head register that the sound vibrates in their heads rather than their chests. Even though this has been found to be untrue by doctors, the term "head voice" is still very common.
"Hook"	A "slang" word referring to that one line of lyric and music designed to "catch" the listener's interest and to make the song stand out.
"Improvise"	To perform or speak without preparation; to make something up, invent, or arrange offhand; to fabricate out of what is conveniently on hand.
"Inter-Audience Bond"	The bond formed between the artist and the audience.

"Intra-Audience Bond"	The bond formed between and among audience members.
"Interpretation"	A performer's distinctive personal version of a song.
"Isolation of Movement"	To perform with a motion or movement which utilizes only one principal body part. You have "isolated" or "set apart" that one body part from the rest of your body. I.e., For a right shoulder roll, your right shoulder goes up and back and down and around to the front. Yes, your arm and hand follows the shoulder in its movement, but the motion is principally that of the shoulder; an isolation of movement of the shoulder. Position Two – "Left Pivot," start in Position One, then pivot (swivel) your left foot slightly to the left so that your left heel is pointing to the middle or instep of your right foot. Position Three – "Right Pivot," start in Position One, then pivot (swivel) your right foot slightly to the right so that your right heel is pointing to the middle or instep of your left foot
"Karaoke"	Karaoke is believed to have originated in a small bar in Japan. The in-house band recorded their music onto tape and, if they were not present, the singer would just sing along to the tape. The word Karaoke was written on the tape, "Kara" meaning missing and "Oke" meaning band or orchestra. -ORIGIN Japanese: kara, void empty + oke (sutora), orchestra (from English orchestra) Latin.
"Lunge"	The act of positioning yourself to stand or perform momentarily with one knee bent and the other leg straight. How large or small your lunge is depends upon how far your feet are apart. Side lunges or front lunges. (Stay balanced!)
"Monotone"	1. A succession of sounds or words uttered in a single tone of voice. 2. Musically, a single tone repeated with different words. 3. Sameness or dull repetition in sound, style, manner, or color. - ORIGIN Greek.
"Patter"	Your verbal, but non-singing, chat with your audience. Usually occurs between songs, during a song's introduction, or during the instrumental.

"Pendulum"	A weight hung from a fixed point so that it can swing freely, especially one regulating the mechanism of a clock. – ORIGIN Latin, 'thing hanging down'.
"Persona"	You, the entertainer, as opposed to you, in real life. Your portrayal of you as the performer. Sometimes referred to as your "on stage persona."
"Phrase"	A group of words (lyrics) that functions as a single unit. -ORIGIN Greek.
"Phraseology"	In linguistics, phraseology describes the context in which a word is used. This often includes typical usages and/or sequences, such as idioms, phrasal verbs, and multi-word units. In music, phraseology describes the integration of the lyrics and the music, sometimes referred to as the "text and tune."
"Phrasing"	The manner, including timing, in which the lyrics of the song are expressed.
"Pitch"	The property of sound that varies with variation in the frequency of vibration. The relative position of a tone within a range of musical sounds, as determined by the tone's quality. – ORIGIN English.
"Pivot"	A movement of the feet, turning on the ball or balls of the feet.
"Poise"	1. A hold in equilibrium; balance. Freedom from affectation or embarrassment; composure. -ORIGIN Latin. 2. Social poise is to demonstrate grace, tact, self composure, dignity, refinement, and/or self-confident manner.
"Product"	A commodity offered for sale: You, the singer, performer, and/or entertainer. You are the "goods;" an article of commerce.
"Real Life"	You, and your way of being, as opposed to you, the performer of song.

"Repertoire"	The stock of songs that a singer is prepared to perform. -ORIGIN Old French from Late Latin.
"Rhythm"	The variation of the duration of sounds over time. -ORIGIN Greek = tempo.
"Scenario"	A brief description of an event or a series of events. -ORIGIN Italian, that which is pinned to the scenery.
"Showmanship"	The ability to present yourself, as an entertainer, and your song in an attractive way.
"Silhouette"	It is the outline view of a person and a featureless interior.
"Stage Left"	The area of the stage to the left of center stage when facing your audience. Your left hand when you face your audience.
"Stage Right"	The area of the stage to the right of center stage when facing your audience. Your right hand when you face your audience.
"Sternum"	A human's chest or breastbone; the long, flat bone located in the center of your thorax (chest). -ORIGIN Greek, sternon, 'chest'.
"Subtext"	The implicit meaning or theme of a song; an underlying theme or an implied relationship between the performer and the song. The subtext of a song is not explicitly stated, but often interpreted by fans based upon the singer's performance. Subtext is particularly helpful during the intro, musical phrases, instrumental, and outro of a song.
"Sync"	From the word synchronous; meaning to adjust two or more things to go together in time or manner.
"Time Signature"	The time signatures (also called meter signatures) tell the singer and musicians how many beats per measure there are in the song, and what kind of note gets the beat.

"Tracks"	Music or pieces of music on a CD or other musical recording, usually without the lead vocals.
"Up Stage"	(1) At or toward the rear of a theatrical stage; (2) away from a motion-picture or television camera.
"Yawn"	To open the mouth wide with a deep inhalation.
"Verse"	In popular music, a verse is like a poetic stanza, that usually maintains the same form but with different words. The verse is often sharply contrasted with the chorus or refrains, which usually assume a higher level of dynamics and activity, often with added instruments.
"Vibrato"	a pulsating effect in an instrumental or vocal tone produced by slight and rapid variations in pitch
"Vitality"	Verve or an energetic style. Physical or intellectual vigor.
"Vowel"	1. The following letters are vowels: a, e, i, o, u, and sometimes h. As a general rule, you should pronounce the vowels in a song with their short vowel sound and not their long vowel sound. 2. The short vowel sounds are: a - apple, e - egg, i - insect, o - orange, and u - umbrella and usually symbolized with a short convex curve (˘) above the vowel. 3. The long vowel sounds are usually symbolized with a short straight line (¯) above the vowel. 4. The long sounds are: a - plane, e - key, I - nine, o - bone, and u - tuba.

ABOUT THE AUTHOR

The **Dynamic Song Performance** Skills method begins by reinforcing successful performance skills while re-directing unsuccessful ones. Pepper Jay and her coaching partner, John Michael Ferrari, guide students through the general aspects of vocal, physical, emotional, and mental song performance skills required of a successful professional singer, performer, recording artist and entertainer. Pepper Jay then hones the student's skills to perfection while teaching audience psychology skills. Each student receives customized coaching depending upon their talents and their expressed goals.

What makes a singer a star? Pepper drills into students' heads that there are many excellent singers who never "make it." Over several decades, Pepper Jay has developed powerful song performance guidelines that, when followed by talent who remain true to themselves, result in impressive success.

This text, Dynamic Performance Skills, The Singers Bible, is a guide to the fundamentals of song performance, directed to both the novice singer with dreams of fame and fortune, as well as the professional singer who wants to increase mastery of song performance skills and be at the top of their craft.

Pepper Jay

Pepper Jay's best friend when she was little was her Grandma Lida. And Grandma's best friend was Sophie Tucker, the "last of the great hot mamas." From 5 to 15 years old, Pepper Jay spent her weekends at the Coconut Grove, Moulin Rouge (Hollywood), Brown Derby, Sands Hotel and Flamingo Hotel (Las Vegas; when the Flamingo tower in front was a moving display of pink and white lights), and numerous other entertainment venues. Grandma loved good food and great entertainment. Old Blue Eyes, Sammy, Dean, Angie, Jimmy Durante, and of course, Sophie, were just a few of the acts Pepper Jay enjoyed as a child.

Pepper Jay began her own performance career at about age 7 by appearing in television sitcoms, such as "The Real McCoys," and performing on stage in school, at St. Andrews Playground (the neighborhood park), and in community theater. Pepper acted, danced and played her accordion for numerous fund-raisers and charities, such as the City of Hope.

A high school drop out, Pepper Jay graduated from El Camino College with an AA Degree and with a BA from San Diego State University. After a year of graduate school, she began teaching in public schools, earning a lifetime teaching credential from the State of California. Pepper taught several subjects for the Los Angeles Unified School District including drama, dance, health education, Spanish, and physical education. During the 1970's, she taught at Hollywood High School, John Muir Junior High School, and, Crenshaw High School, where she was in charge of coordinating and producing shows by the "drill team."

Although Pepper Jay completed her pubic teaching career in 1983, when she earned a JD from the University of San Diego and then practiced law for more than thirty years, she continued her private teaching, coaching, and speaking engagements. Pepper continues to coach performance skills for actors, singers, public speakers, lawyers; anyone required to be in front of cameras or an audience. Also, Pepper speaks about performance skills at film festivals, to acting schools, and at conventions throughout the United States.

In 1990, Pepper Jay became John Michael Ferrari's performance coach. In 1991, they partnered to create the Pepper J. Productions entertainment company, now known as Pepper Jay Productions LLC. In 1993, Pepper created the Working Actors Group, offering free on-camera and cold reading workshops to working union actors. In 2003, John joined Pepper in the private coaching of singers and actors.

Pepper Jay is a member of some amazing organizations, including the All Cities Resourse Group (thank you Eric Shaw) and Arts 4 Peace (thank you Munni Irone).

Today, Pepper Jay is found on both sides of the camera. Please check her out on IMDB.com

Pepper Jay is also the publisher and producer of the Actors Reporter, Actors Entertainment, and Actors Radio, channels on the Actors Podcast Network. Actors Reporter is an American entertainment-trade online magazine about working actors, singers, and others in the entertainment industry (with shows airing both on the Internet and Cable). Some of the shows on the Actors Podcast Network include Acting in Style, Actors Day in LA, G-d in Hollywood, Johnny Shorts, Models Best Friend, Savoring the Sweetness, Sidebeat Music, The Stevie D. Show, The EZ Show, and Tinsel on the Town, plus a variety of interview shows, including ,Motivational

Dynamic Song Performance

Chat, Interviews., and ActorsE Chat (Actors Entertainment on IMDb), a M-F live hour-long chat show. As of the writing of this text, ActorsE Chat is in its 6th season, with more than 1,200 entertainment industry guests, and more than 6 million viewers. First and foremost an actress, please visit Pepper Jay on IMDb (that's the Internet Movie Database) to see many of her films, TV, and video game roles.

Pepper Jay
Photo by John Michael Ferrari

Recent song performance students of Pepper Jay and John Michael Ferrari include:

- Allison Iraheta (Winner, Telemundo's Quinceañera 2006; Top 4 "American Idol, Season 8," first album for Jive Records "Just Like You,;" lead singer in band "Halo Circus."

- Nikki Nova (Top 10 "Taiwan Idol 2009," lead singer in band, "Liquid Blue")

- Liquid Blue (Pop Album of the Year 2009 (Supernova) by Los Angeles Music Awards

- Golda Berkman, Teen Opera Singer (2014)

- Gisell (Winner Romantic Division "Premios Talentos 2010")

- Montana Tucker (teen sensation hip-hop dancer and singer)

- Kristen Rose (Miss Tennessee Teen USA 2010)

- Stevie Wright (Top 36 "American Idol, Season 8" 2009; lead singer in "The James Gang")

- Catey Rudoy 2009-2011 actress, comic, singer, and songwriter (Lead in TV variety show pilot "Sparky's" 2011; known as "Cat Ivy," "Creating My Life" (2012)

- Brandon James – West Coast Country (Named a Hot 100 Unsigned Artist 2011/2012 by Music Connection Magazine); Country Album of the Year (21st Annual LA Music Awards)

- LusiaLaBell, singer, dancer, actor (third place on Telemundo's Quinceañera 2006; finals on Star Search (CBS))

Accolades

"This lovely little book contains so much valuable information for the aspiring singer; principles of stage movement, branding, mic technique, patter, gesture, psychology, emotion, and so much more. It explains how to connect with an audience and create performance magic!"

-Lisa Popeil, celebrity voice coach (2013)

"Pepper Jay's ***Dynamic Song Performance*** Skills is great for anyone focused on moving forward with their singing career. Pepper is loved, innovative, and well respected."

-Sam Sarpong aka Future, actor and rapper (2013)

"John and Pepper, I don't know how to thank you both for opening up your hearts to me this week. I've learned so much from you and I will take it with me wherever I go in life. Above all else what I appreciate most is all of your encouragement. The two of you are amazing teachers and I value both of you so much. I am looking forward to Hollywood again, Love"

- Kristen Rose (2011)

"Without the guidance of Pepper Jay and John Michael Ferrari I would not have the success I have today. I love you two!"
Allison Iraheta, (2009) recording artist (Jive Records); Top 4, "American Idol, Season 8" (Fox) (2009); winner, Telemundo's, "Quinceañera" (2006); recording artist and lead vocalist in Halo Circus (Manimal Vinyl) (2013).

"When I first went searching for a performance coach, one was hard to find. There were tons of vocal and instrument teachers, music classes, dance classes, and even theater. But, I couldn't find anyone that knew how to teach what I was looking for: stage performance. Then, I found Pepper and John. They were exactly what I was searching for. I spent weeks with them training and learning. They went through every aspect of performance and answered all my questions. It didn't matter to them that I was singing songs in a different language. The art of performance rings true no matter what language, or genre, for that matter.

I went on to be the first Westerner to make it to the Top 10 on Taiwan Idol, and I have to say that a large part of that is due to what they taught me. No one focuses on the teaching of performance like Pepper Jay and John Michael Ferrari. They really specialize in this area and make a good team. The skills that Pepper Jay shares in this book are something that every performer, at any level, should learn. Everything is covered from A to Z. I highly recommend this to anyone who is looking to get into a career in music or is already a seasoned pro, or anyone who just wants to be better on stage. It's organized and concise but thoroughly explains each idea. Pepper gives you tips, ideas, techniques, exercises, and step-by-step instructions of how-tos.

-Nikki Nova, lead vocalist, Liquid Blue (2013)

"There comes times when you meet people who impact your life. You hope they help you, guide you and provide the knowledge needed to reach your dreams. For me, those amazing and beautiful people inside and out are Pepper Jay and John Michael Ferrari.

With their professional guidance and unique way of teaching, I have become much more skilled in my career as a singer, actress and dancer. I am able to apply what I learn from them to both my career and my personal life as well. Thank you Pepper Jay and John for giving me the confidence and courage to take on whatever this world brings my way." Love Always,

Montana Tucker, (2009) hip-hop singer/dancer (2009)

"Since I've been Pepper Jay and John Ferrari's student, my vocal and performance skills have improved greatly. I've become a more confident performer and learned to step out of my shell. Not only are Pepper and John wonderful second parents to me, I know I can trust them with anything. I always look forward to applying the skills I've gained to my performances."
Stevie Wright, (2009) Top 36 "American Idol, Season 8" (Fox) 2009

"Without Pepper and John's help, I would never know what I could actually be capable of doing in my life."
Catey Rudoy aka "Sparky," (2010) actress, comic singer, and songwriter.

"You two are the best. Thank you John Ferrari and Pepper Jay!"
Melinda del Toro, (2008) international singer & performer

"I never liked looking at myself perform. I couldn't believe how fast my singing performance skills improved with John and Pepper's guidance and what they showed me using the video camera. My vocal teachers couldn't communicate to me what was needed. ***Dynamic Song Performance*** works and it's wonderful. Thank you John and Pepper".
Kaylene Peoples (1999) producer, composer, arranger, conductor, recording artist, accomplished musician, and former Miss California. All Jazzed Up" on Boogsey Music (2005)

"Each session with John and Pepper, I was more impressed with their talent, creativity, and vision. Their warmth and optimism are inspiring. Through their deep understanding of people, they helped me discover completely new aspects of myself whether it be through photographs, scenes, or vocals. Working with John and Pepper was fun, enlightening, and always NEW!"
Carly Oates, actor/model (2001)

"Pepper has been an inspiration to me. Her positive attitude, obvious love for "the work" and bountiful energy are all beacons of light for me. I love working with her!
Gretchen Weiss, actress/ singer. (Sept 2001)

"Amazing. For 30 years I thought I couldn't sing. John and Pepper made singing really easy and fun. A great time!"

Thereza Ellis, actor (1998)

"John Michael Ferrari is A Survivor In The Spotlight"
... and "a respected song performance and acting coach."
Elias Stimac, Karaoke Scene Magazine (Oct/Nov 1998)

The Tolucan calls our Johnny Ferrari "a crooner" with a "smooth as silk" voice.
- The Tolucan, "Easing on the Eyes," September 6, 1995)

Dynamic Song Performance

"Dear John, You are my favorite partner in crime ... I couldn't have asked for more".
Mary Elizabeth McGlynn, (1994) actor, singer, voiceover director ("Waiting For You", "Letter ' from The Lost Days", "You're Not Here", "Invisible Man")

The **Los Angeles Times** reports that John Michael is "reminiscent of Sammy Davis Jr. or the early Bobby Darin". **(Los Angeles Times, July 9, 1993)**

RJ (1992-2013)
Photo by John Michael Ferrari

Bibliography and References

Although not quoted, Pepper Jay and John Michael Ferrari have shared with you knowledge discovered from the following dynamic personal development gurus. Much of what can be learned from the works of these amazing people will greatly benefit your song performance skills. Don't leave home without them:

Earl Nightingale. Your author believes she has read almost all of the books and writings of Earl Nightingale. As Mr. Nightingale always reminds us, we are what we think! Visit www.earlnightingale.com.

Anthony Robbins. Your author has probably read and listened on tape to all of the books of Anthony "Tony" Robbins. Consider each product from Anthony Robbins to be a "personal development Bible!" An absolute must read is "Awaken the Giant Within: How to take immediate control of your mental, emotional, physical & financial destiny!" by Anthony Robbins. Published 1992, Fireside Simon and Schuster. Visit www.anthonyrobbins.com.

Additional Recommended Reading:
"Yes, I Can: The Sammy Davis Jr. Story, by Sammy Davis Jr, with Burt and Jane Boyar. (Rhino/Wea 1965)

Rolling Stones Article, "One For the Road; Frank Sinatra sang out our soul,"posted May 15, 1998, by Mark A. Mehle

Notes

Notes

Notes

Notes